Target
Get back on track

GRADE 5

Edexcel GCSE (9–1)
Spanish
Writing

Ana Kolkowska, Libby Mitchell

Pearson

Published by Pearson Education Limited, 80 Strand, London, WC2R ORL.

www.pearsonschoolsandfecolleges.co.uk

Copies of official specifications for all Pearson qualifications may be found on the website: qualifications.pearson.com

Text © Pearson Education Limited 2017
Produced by Out of House Publishing
Typeset by Newgen KnowledgeWorks Pvt. Ltd., Chennai, India

The rights of Ana Kolkowska and Libby Mitchell to be identified as authors of this work have been asserted by them in accordance with the Copyright, Designs and Patents Act 1988.

First published 2017

20 19 18
10 9 8 7 6 5 4 3 2

British Library Cataloguing in Publication Data
A catalogue record for this book is available from the British Library

ISBN 978 0435 18908 2

Printed in Slovakia by Neografia

Acknowledgements
The publisher would like to thank the following individuals and organisations for permission to reproduce their photographs:

(Key: b-bottom; c-centre; l-left; r-right; t-top)

Shutterstock: Oneinchpunch 1, 2, 3t, 6, View Apart 3b, Lucky Business 5, Monkey Business Images 7, bikeriderlondon 8

All other images © Pearson Education

Note from the publisher
Pearson has robust editorial processes, including answer and fact checks, to ensure the accuracy of the content in this publication, and every effort is made to ensure this publication is free of errors. We are, however, only human, and occasionally errors do occur. Pearson is not liable for any misunderstandings that arise as a result of errors in this publication, but it is our priority to ensure that the content is accurate. If you spot an error, please do contact us resourcescorrections@pearson.com so we can make sure it is corrected.

 This workbook has been developed using the Pearson Progression Map and Scale for Spanish.

To find out more about the Progression Scale for Spanish and to see how it relates to indicative GCSE 9–1 grades go to www.pearsonschools.co.uk/ProgressionServices

Helping you to formulate grade predictions, apply interventions and track progress.

Any reference to indicative grades in the Pearson Target Workbooks and Pearson Progression Services is not to be used as an accurate indicator of how a student will be awarded a grade for their GCSE exams.

You have told us that mapping the Steps from the Pearson Progression Maps to indicative grades will make it simpler for you to accumulate the evidence to formulate your own grade predictions, apply any interventions and track student progress. We're really excited about this work and its potential for helping teachers and students. It is, however, important to understand that this mapping is for guidance only to support teachers' own predictions of progress and is not an accurate predictor of grades.

Our Pearson Progression Scale is criterion referenced. If a student can perform a task or demonstrate a skill, we say they are working at a certain Step according to the criteria. Teachers can mark assessments and issue results with reference to these criteria which do not depend on the wider cohort in any given year. For GCSE exams however, all Awarding Organisations set the grade boundaries with reference to the strength of the cohort in any given year. For more information about how this works please visit: https://qualifications.pearson.com/en/support/support-topics/results-certification/understanding-marks-and-grades.html/Teacher

Contents

1 Writing interesting descriptions

Get started 1

1 How do I make my descriptions more interesting? 3

2 How do I make my descriptions more varied? 4

3 How do I write descriptions more accurately? 5

Sample response 6

Your turn! 7

Review your skills 8

2 Giving and explaining your opinions

Get started 9

1 How do I make my opinions relevant to the topic? ... 11

2 How do I add detail to my opinions? 12

3 How do I justify my opinions convincingly? 13

Sample response 14

Your turn! 15

Review your skills 16

3 Making your meaning clear

Get started 17

1 How do I write clear sentences in Spanish? 19

2 How do I write natural-sounding Spanish? 20

3 How do I use the right style? 21

Sample response 22

Your turn! 23

Review your skills 24

4 Writing effectively about the past

Get started 25

1 How do I use opportunities to write about the past? ... 27

2 How do I vary references to the past for added interest? ... 28

3 How do I make sure I use the past tense correctly? ... 29

Sample response 30

Your turn! 31

Review your skills 32

5 Writing effectively about the future

Get started 33

1 How do I use opportunities to write about the future? ... 35

2 How do I use the future tense correctly? 36

3 How do I vary references to the future for added interest? ... 37

Sample response 38

Your turn! 39

Review your skills 40

6 Choosing and linking your ideas

Get started 41

1 How do I choose what I want to say? 43

2 How do I organise my answer? 44

3 How do I link my ideas logically? 45

Sample response 46

Your turn! 47

Review your skills 48

7 Improving your accuracy

Get started 49

1 How do I write correct verb forms? 51

2 How do I check agreements? 52

3 How do I improve my spelling? 53

Sample response 54

Your turn! 55

Review your skills 56

8 Translating into Spanish

Get started 57

1 How do I avoid translating word for word? 59

2 How do I use the correct Spanish equivalents for certain verbs and phrases? ... 60

3 How do I make sure my translation is accurate? ... 61

Sample response 62

Your turn! 63

Review your skills 64

9 Using impressive language

Get started 65

1 How do I make sure I use interesting vocabulary? ... 67

2 How do I use grammar to best effect? 68

3 How do I create opportunities to use more complex language? ... 69

Sample response 70

Your turn! 71

Review your skills 72

Answers 73

① Writing interesting descriptions

This unit will help you learn how to write interesting descriptions. The skills you will build are to:

• make your descriptions more interesting

• make your descriptions more varied

• write descriptions more accurately.

In the exam, you will be asked to tackle a writing task such as the one below. This unit will prepare you to write your own response to this question.

Exam-style question

Estás de vacaciones en España. Publicas esta foto en las redes sociales para tus amigos.

Describe la foto **y** da tu opinión sobre las vacaciones en la ciudad.

Escribe aproximadamente 20–30 palabras **en español**. (12 marks)

The three key questions in the **skills boosts** will help you to improve your descriptions. (You will work on the second part of the question, giving your opinion, in Unit 2.)

 1 How do I make my descriptions more interesting?

 2 How do I make my descriptions more varied?

 3 How do I write descriptions more accurately?

Look at the sample student answer on the next page.

Look at one student's description of the photo from the exam-style question.

Exam style question

Describe la foto y da tu opinión sobre las vacaciones en la ciudad.

En esta foto hay unos jóvenes en una ciudad. Hace sol. Creo que es verano. Están de vacaciones. En mi opinión, las vacaciones en una ciudad son divertidas porque hay mucho que hacer.

(1) Now read these statements in English referring to the student's description. Two of them are wrong. Mark a cross (×) next to the incorrect statements.

a It is a cloudy day.

b The writer thinks it is summer.

c The writer likes going on holiday in a city.

d The writer thinks the people are working there.

e The writer thinks there are plenty of things to do in a city.

(2) Look carefully at each part of the student's description. Match (✏) each Spanish phrase with the English word or phrase that describes it.

A en una ciudad	a what the weather is like
B Hace sol.	b opinion
C porque hay mucho que hacer	c where they are
D unos jóvenes	d opinion
E las vacaciones en una ciudad son divertidas	e who is in the photo
F Creo que es verano.	f reason

(3) Look again at the English words and phrases a–f above. Write (✏) them below in the order they appear in the student's description.

1 *who is in the photo*

2 ....

3 ....

4 ....

5 ....

6 ....

1 How do I make my descriptions more interesting?

In order to add interest to your descriptions you need to expand your descriptive vocabulary.

Look again at the exam-style question.

Exam style question

Describe la foto y da tu opinión sobre las vacaciones en la ciudad.

① You can improve your descriptions by using adjectives to add interest. Look at the Spanish adjectives in the box below. Choose those which best describe people, those which are used for places, and those used for holidays, and write ✐ them in the table underneath. Some adjectives may fit in more than one category.

Remember! Adjectives agree with what they describe.
- *antiguo, antigua, antiguos, antiguas*
- *inolvidable, inolvidables*
- *azul, azules*

histórico inolvidable turístico joven activo cómodo mayor
relajante simpático malo bonito barato preocupado
lujoso bueno contento desastroso moderno triste ruidoso

Personas	Lugares	Vacaciones
	turístico	

② Look at the photo below and read one student's description of it. Complete ✐ the description using the appropriate words from the box. Don't forget to make the adjectives agree.

bueno   bonito   inolvidable   contento

En esta foto hay unos jóvenes .... Están en

una playa .... Hace ....

tiempo. Son unas vacaciones ....

③ Now it's your turn. On paper, write ✐ two sentences of your own to describe the photo in ②.

Skills boost

② How do I make my descriptions more varied?

To add variety to your descriptions you should use connectives, adverbs and prepositions of place to link and develop your writing.

① Look again at the first photo on page 3. Then read this sample student answer. There are two options in bold for each detail. Circle Ⓐ the appropriate option in each case.

> En esta foto **en el centro / a la izquierda** hay unos jóvenes en una ciudad **turismo / turística**. Hace **poco / mucho** sol. Creo que es verano **y / pero** están de vacaciones. En mi opinión, las vacaciones en una ciudad son **grandes / muy** divertidas porque **siempre / nunca** hay mucho que hacer.

Prepositions		Connectives		Adverbs	
a la derecha	on the right	pero	but	siempre	always
a la izquierda	on the left	y	and	nunca	never
en el centro	in the centre	además	besides	a veces	sometimes
debajo	under	por eso	so	muy	very
sobre	on	también	also		
delante	in front	primero	first		
detrás	behind	después	after		
entre	between	finalmente	finally		

② Fill ✎ the gaps in the sentences below using an appropriate word/phrase from the box.

> muy   también   mucho   porque   en el centro   debajo   por eso   a la izquierda

  ⓐ El castillo está .... de la foto.

  ⓑ Hace .... frío en invierno.

  ⓒ Hay un chico .... y una chica a la derecha.

  ⓓ .... hay una chica en una bicicleta.

  ⓔ En mi opinión, las vacaciones en la playa son .... aburridas.

  ⓕ En la foto hay un perro .... de la mesa.

  ⓖ Prefiero ir a España en verano .... me gusta el sol.

  ⓗ Me gusta ir de compras, ... voy a la ciudad.

③ Look again at the second photo on page 3. Write ✎ your own description of the photo, adding connectives, adverbs and prepositions of place.

....

....

....

....

....

3 How do I write descriptions more accurately?

To write descriptions accurately in Spanish you must check agreements, particularly relating to gender, number and subject-verb.

1 Look again at the sample student answer from page 2.

> En esta foto hay unos jóvenes en una ciudad. Hace sol. Creo que es verano. Están de vacaciones. En mi opinión, las vacaciones en una ciudad son divertidas porque hay mucho que hacer.

a The table below contains four gender-number categories. Find a phrase or word in the text for each of these categories and write ✎ them in the table.

b How did you decide which one to choose? Add ✎ a note to each of the examples you have chosen.

	Phrase/word in text	Note
masculine singular:		
masculine plural:		
feminine singular:	una ciudad	'una' is the feminine singular word for 'a'
feminine plural:		

2 The subject and the verb need to agree with each other. Complete ✎ the sentences below with the correct form of the verb in brackets. Use the present tense.

a El hotel (ser) .... muy cómodo.

b Las vacaciones de esquí (ser) .... activas.

c La chica (llevar) .... unas zapatillas deportivas.

d Los jóvenes (estar) .... en el campo.

e El grupo (comer) .... al aire libre.

f El chico (comprar) .... un recuerdo típico.

g El hombre (hablar) .... con el recepcionista.

h La familia (visitar) .... el castillo.

Regular present tense verb endings

	3rd person singular (he/she/it)	3rd person plural (they)
-ar (e.g. nadar)	nada	nadan
-er (e.g. beber)	bebe	beben
-ir (e.g. vivir)	vive	viven

Two important irregular verbs in present tense

ser	es	son
estar	está	están

3 Look at the photo and read the description next to it. The text contains four mistakes.

> Las chicas está en un parque. Hace muchas sol. Practicamos yoga. Creo que es divertidas.

a Find and circle Ⓐ each mistake.

b Now write ✎ the correct version.

....

....

....

....

Sample response

To improve your descriptions, you need to:

- make them more interesting
- make them more varied
- write them more accurately.

Look again at the exam-style writing task from page 1.

Look again at the exam-style writing task from page 1.

Exam-style question

Estás de vacaciones en España. Publicas esta foto en las redes sociales para tus amigos.

Describe la foto **y** da tu opinión sobre las vacaciones en la ciudad.

Escribe aproximadamente 20–30 palabras **en español**. **(12 marks)**

Now look at one student's answer to the question.

> *Hay chicos. Hace sol. Es verano. En mi opinión, las vacaciones en una ciudad son aburridas.*

1. Tick ✓ which of the following are featured in this student's answer.

   a prepositions of place ☐   c adverbs ☐

   b adjectives ☐   d connectives ☐

2. Write ✏ whether you think this student has written a convincing answer to the task. Justify your answer.

   ....

   ....

   ....

   ....

3. Think about how you could improve this student's response. Rewrite ✏ the answer, adding details to make it more interesting.

   ....

   ....

   ....

   ....

Your turn!

You are now going to plan and write your response to the following exam-style task.

Publicas esta foto en las redes sociales para tus amigos.

Describe la foto **y** da tu opinión sobre las vacaciones en invierno.

Escribe aproximadamente 20–30 palabras **en español**.

(12 marks)

(1) Plan your answer. Fill in 🖉 the table below in English.

description	notes
who is in the photo:	
where they are:	
what the weather is like:	
what they are doing:	
your opinion:	

(2) Now write 🖉 your response to the above exam-style question. Once you have finished, read through your answers using the checklist.

....

....

....

....

....

Checklist In my answer do I ...	✓
use precise and varied vocabulary?	
use prepositions of place?	
use connectives?	
use adjectives?	
use adverbs?	
write accurately (verbs, adjectives)?	

....

....

Review your skills

Check up

Review your response to the exam-style question on page 7. Tick ⊘ the column to show how well you think you have done each of the following.

	Not quite ⊘	Nearly there ⊘	Got it! ⊘
made descriptions more interesting	☐	☐	☐
made descriptions more varied	☐	☐	☐
written descriptions more accurately	☐	☐	☐

Need more practice?

On paper, plan and write 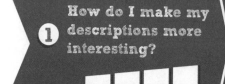 your response to the exam-style task below.

Exam-style question

Practicas voleibol en tus vacaciones. Publicas esta foto en las redes sociales para tus amigos.

Describe la foto **y** da tu opinión sobre practicar deportes en la playa.

Escribe aproximadamente 20–30 palabras **en español**.

(12 marks)

How confident do you feel about each of these **skills?** Colour in ✏ the bars.

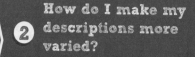

1 How do I make my descriptions more interesting?

2 How do I make my descriptions more varied?

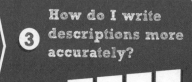

3 How do I write descriptions more accurately?

② Giving and explaining your opinions

This unit will help you learn how to give convincing opinions. The skills you will build are to:

• make your opinions relevant to the topic

• add detail to your opinions

• justify your opinions.

In the exam, you will be asked to tackle writing tasks such as the two below. This unit will prepare you to plan and write your own responses to these questions. As part of these tasks, you have to give opinions.

Exam-style question

Un instituto inglés

Su profesor le ha pedido escribir un artículo para una revista de estudiantes españoles sobre la vida en un instituto inglés.

Escriba usted el artículo con la información siguiente:

• una descripción de su instituto

• cuáles son sus asignaturas favoritas

• lo mejor de su instituto

• qué hará la semana que viene para el día del deporte.

Escriba aproximadamente 40–50 palabras **en español**.   (16 marks)

Exam-style question

Mi instituto

Tu amigo Alex quiere visitar tu instituto y te envía unas preguntas.

Escríbele una respuesta a Alex.

Debes incluir los puntos siguientes:

• cómo son tus profesores

• tu opinión sobre tu uniforme

• las actividades extraescolares que hiciste la semana pasada

• lo que vas a hacer durante su visita al instituto.

Escribe aproximadamente 80–90 palabras **en español**.   (20 marks)

The three key questions in the **skills boosts** will help you to improve how you express your opinions.

 1 How do I make my opinions relevant to the topic?   **2** How do I add detail to my opinions?   **3** How do I justify my opinions convincingly?

Look at the sample student answers on the next page.

(1) First, check you understand key information in the bullet points of both exam-style questions on page 9. On paper, write 🖊 the English equivalent of the words **in bold**.

Exam-style question

- una descripción de su **instituto**
- cuáles son sus **asignaturas favoritas**
- **lo mejor** de su instituto
- **qué hará la semana que viene** para el día del deporte.

Exam-style question

- cómo son tus **profesores**
- tu **opinión** sobre tu **uniforme**
- las **actividades extraescolares** que hiciste **la semana pasada**
- lo que **vas a hacer** durante **su visita al instituto**.

(2) **a** Read sample answer A and the sentences below. Put a cross ⊗ in the box next to the incorrect sentences.

A

> Mi instituto se llama St Claire's School, es privado y mixto. Está muy cerca de Londres. Me gustan mucho las matemáticas y las ciencias porque los profesores son excelentes. Lo mejor de mi instituto es que hay un polideportivo inmenso porque practico muchos deportes. La semana que viene voy a participar en un torneo de tenis de mesa.

i   The school is a mixed private school. ☐

ii   It is quite far from London. ☐

iii The student likes Biology and English. ☐

iv   The sport centre is quite small. ☐

v   The student will go on a trip next week. ☐

b Read sample answer B and the sentences below. Put a cross ⊗ in the box next to the incorrect sentences.

B

> Hola, Alex:
>
> Creo que mis profesores son simpáticos. Me gusta mi profesor de historia porque es muy divertido.
>
> En mi instituto tengo que llevar uniforme. No me gusta nada porque es incómodo, pero es práctico.
>
> Me encantan las actividades extraescolares porque hay mucho para elegir. La semana pasada fui al club de teatro y también hice natación. ¡Fue superdivertido!
>
> Durante tu visita vamos a asistir a distintas clases y creo que te van a gustar mucho. Por la tarde vamos a ver una obra de teatro muy buena con mis compañeros del club.

i   The student doesn't get on with his teachers because they are strict. ☐

ii   They have to wear uniform at school. ☐

iii The student thinks wearing a uniform is boring. ☐

iv   Last week he went swimming. ☐

v   They will go to see a play in the afternoon. ☐

How do I make my opinions relevant to the topic?

Look at these sentences:

Positive opinions	Negative opinions
Me gusta la informática. **Es guay.**	No me gusta la comida. **Es fatal.**
Me encanta practicar la natación. **Es guay.**	Odio la química. **Es fatal.**

Es guay and *Es fatal* are opinions that could apply to almost any topic. To make your writing more interesting, find **more precise adjectives** to express your opinions.

(1) Learn adjectives with their opposites. Look at the list below and write 🖉 the English equivalent of each pair of Spanish adjectives, using the Spanish sentence below each pair to help you.

a delicioso / asqueroso: *delicious / disgusting*

La comida en el comedor del instituto es **deliciosa**! ¡Me encanta!

b fuerte / débil: ....

Después de jugar al baloncesto, estoy muy **débil**.

c inteligente / tonto: ....

Mi primo Leo es muy **inteligente**; siempre saca notas altas.

d complicado / simple: ....

Me interesa la tecnología, pero es muy **complicada**.

e perezoso / trabajador: ....

Mi hermano nunca hace los deberes; es muy **perezoso**.

f injusto / justo: ....

Es muy **injusto** tener que llevar uniforme; ¡no me gusta nada!

g tranquilo / ruidoso:

....

Lo mejor de la clase de arte es que es muy **tranquilo**; no hay mucho ruido.

h limpio / sucio: ....

Esta clase está muy **sucia**; ¡hay basura en el suelo!

(2) Write 🖉 your opinion about the following, using some of the adjectives above.

> Remember that you need to consider whether the word is masculine or feminine, singular or plural when using adjectives in Spanish.

a The food at your school

En mi opinión, ...

b Your uniform

Pienso que ....

c One of your teachers

Creo que ....

d One of your subjects at school

Desde mi punto de vista, ...

2 **How do I add detail to my opinions?**

Expand the ways you give opinions by:
- using varied phrases, not just *me gusta* and *no me gusta*
- giving opinions about events in the past, too, by using *fue*.

1 Read these opinions about school life. Underline (A) the phrases that introduce a positive opinion and circle (A) the phrases that introduce a negative opinion.

> Lo mejor de mi instituto es que es moderno y las instalaciones son nuevas. Pero lo peor es que
> es demasiado grande. Me mola el polideportivo porque está bien equipado, pero por desgracia
> no hay piscina. Me encantan los profesores, pero ponen muchos deberes. ¡Qué horror! Detesto el
> uniforme porque es muy formal. Odio la corbata en particular. Me chifla la variedad de actividades
> extraescolares y toco el violín en la orquesta. ¡Es superdivertido! Me gustó mucho participar en un
> concurso nacional el trimestre pasado. No ganamos, pero ¡fue flipante!

2 Fill the gaps (✏) in the following paragraph, choosing the correct opinions and reasons from the box underneath.

.... las actividades en mi instituto porque son .... y te ayudan

a .... Los jueves voy al club de natación. Voy desde hace un año. ....

porque el trimestre pasado .... También toco el violín en la

orquestra. .... , pero no voy a continuar el año que viene porque ....

| aprender cosas nuevas | me chiflan | gané un trofeo | no tengo tiempo | variadas |
| me encanta | es creativo | ¡Fue genial! |

3 Write (✏) about your extracurricular activities. Give your opinions and mention something you did in the past. Use as many phrases from pages 11 and 12 as you can. Try not to repeat any adjectives!

....

....

....

....

....

....

....

....

③ How do I justify my opinions convincingly?

Your opinions will sound more convincing if:
- you reinforce them by using qualifiers and adverbs
- you justify them by using connectives, such as *porque*, and by giving examples.

① Read this text about a school trip. Circle Ⓐ the qualifiers and adverbs that are used to make the opinions more convincing.

> *Durante las vacaciones fui a Londres con mi clase de español y participamos en un intercambio. Creo que los intercambios son muy buenos porque te ayudan a aprender más inglés. Me alojé en la casa de mi compañera inglesa, Sofie. Desafortunadamente la visita fue bastante difícil porque no hablo bien el inglés y la familia era un poco antipática. También visitamos el centro pero, en mi opinión, Londres es demasiado caro para estudiantes como nosotros.*

Qualifiers and adverbs to reinforce your opinions:

bastante	*quite, rather*
bien	*well, good*
demasiado	*too*
desafortunadamente	*unfortunately*
mal	*bad, badly*
más	*more*
menos	*less*
mucho	*a lot*
muy	*very*
un poco	*a bit, a little*

② Add ✎ appropriate qualifiers and adverbs to fill the gaps in these opinions. Try not to repeat any!

> *Durante el intercambio visitamos el instituto de nuestros compañeros. Los estudiantes ingleses tienen que llevar uniforme. ¡Qué horror! Creo que el uniforme es .... feo y .... formal. Las clases eran .... largas y los profesores eran .... estrictos. Comimos en el comedor y pienso que la comida inglesa es .... variada que la comida española. Me gustó .... la experiencia.*

In the longer exam question (80–90 words), try to justify your opinion by giving a reason. You can introduce that reason with *porque* and add an example with *por ejemplo*.

③ Link up ✎ these opinions, reasons and examples in ways that make sense.

opinions	reasons	examples
a No me gusta llevar uniforme	porque te ayuda a mejorar tu técnica.	La corbata, por ejemplo, no es práctica.
b La comida en el comedor es buena	porque aprendes cosas nuevas.	Por ejemplo, el trimestre pasado gané un trofeo.
c Me mola ir a los clubs extraescolares	porque es variada.	Los postres, por ejemplo, son deliciosos.
d Es flipante participar en concursos	porque es incómodo.	Por ejemplo, el año pasado aprendí a tocar la guitarra.

Sample response

To write more convincing opinions, you need to:

- use more precise adjectives
- use varied phrases, not just *me gusta* and *no me gusta*, and give opinions about events in the past as well as the present
- reinforce your opinions by using qualifiers and adverbs, by giving reasons using *porque*, and by adding examples.

Now look again at the second exam-style question on page 9. Read this student's answer to the question.

> Los profesores de mi instituto no me gustan nada. Las asignaturas son muy aburridas y las clases también son aburridas.
>
> Pienso que llevo un uniforme bastante cómodo. Llevo una camisa blanca, corbata a rayas, pantalón gris y zapatos negros. Un jersey azul.
>
> Las actividades extraescolares son variadas. Hay mucho para hacer. Me gusta jugar al baloncesto, al hockey y al tenis. Hay una piscina grande.
>
> Durante tu visita, creo que vamos a ir a una excursión con la clase. En mi opinión va a ser muy guay.

(1) Write down (✎) whether you think the opinions given in this sample answer are convincing. Justify your answer.

....

....

....

(2) Look at how you can transform an opinion into a convincing opinion. Compare the first two sentences of the student's response above with the version written by another student below. Look at the adjectives and qualifiers this student uses, and how the reasons and examples make their opinions more convincing. Then rewrite (✎) the rest of the sample answer.

> Los profesores de mi instituto no me gustan nada porque son estrictos, muy antipáticos y las asignaturas son muy aburridas. Las clases son poco interesantes porque nunca jugamos o hacemos algo diferente. ¡Es horroroso!

....

....

....

....

....

....

Your turn!

You are now going to plan and write your response to one or both of the exam-style tasks on page 9.

to one or both of the exam-style tasks on page 9.

Exam-style question

Un instituto inglés

Su profesor le ha pedido escribir un artículo para una revista de estudiantes españoles sobre la vida en un instituto inglés. Escriba usted el artículo con la información siguiente:

- una descripción de su instituto
- cuáles son sus asignaturas favoritas
- lo mejor de su instituto
- qué hará la semana que viene para el día del deporte.

Escriba aproximadamente 40–50 palabras **en español**.

Exam-style question

Mi instituto

Tu amigo Alex quiere visitar tu instituto y te envía unas preguntas. Escríbele una respuesta a Alex.

Debes incluir ...

- cómo son tus profesores
- tu opinión sobre tu uniforme
- las actividades extraescolares que hiciste la semana pasada
- lo que vas a hacer durante su visita al instituto.

Escribe aproximadamente 80–90 palabras **en español**.

(1) Before you start writing your answers, plan your responses carefully. Note down ✏️ on paper answers to the following questions to help you.

  (a) Which tenses do you have to use to answer each of the bullet points?

  (b) What key vocabulary will you need to answer each bullet point?

  (c) Where do you have to state opinions?

(2) Now choose which question you want to answer and write ✏️ your response. Once you have finished, read through and check your work.

Checklist In my answer do I ...		✓
answer all the bullet points?		
use precise adjectives, not just *guay* or *fatal?*		
use varied opinion phrases, not just *me gusta / no me gusta?*		
give opinions about events in the past?		
reinforce my opinions with qualifiers and adverbs?	extended writing task only (80–90 words)	
justify my opinions with reasons?		
give examples?		

If you want more practice, tackle the other writing task above, on paper.

Review your skills

Check up

Review your response to the exam-style question you answered on page 15. Tick ⊘ the column to show how well you think you have done each of the following.

	Not quite ⊘	Nearly there ⊘	Got it! ⊘
made opinions relevant to the topic	☐	☐	☐
added detail to opinions	☐	☐	☐
justified opinions	☐	☐	☐

Need more practice?

On paper, plan and write ⊘ your responses to the exam-style tasks below.

Exam-style question

Un intercambio en el instituto

Usted está interesado en un intercambio en un instituto de España.

Escriba usted un correo al director del instituto con esta información:

• qué asignaturas estudia

• describa las instalaciones en su instituto

• las normas en su instituto y su opinión

• dónde se alojará en España.

Escriba aproximadamente 40–50 palabras **en español**.

(16 marks)

Exam-style question

Un viaje escolar

Escribe un blog sobre un viaje escolar a España.

Debes incluir los puntos siguientes:

• una descripción de tu instituto

• lo que hiciste en tu viaje escolar

• lo bueno (lo malo) del viaje

• tu opinión sobre futuros viajes escolares.

Escribe aproximadamente 80–90 palabras **en español**.

(20 marks)

How confident do you feel about each of these **skills**? Colour in ⊘ the bars.

1 How do I make my opinions relevant to the topic?

2 How do I add detail to my opinions?

3 How do I justify my opinions convincingly?

③ Making your meaning clear

This unit will help you learn how to make your meaning clear. The skills you will build are to:

- write clear sentences
- write natural-sounding Spanish
- use the right style.

In the exam, you will be asked to tackle writing tasks such as the two below. This unit will prepare you to plan and write your own responses to these questions.

The three key questions in the **skills boosts** will help you to make your meaning clear.

 1 How do I write clear sentences in Spanish?

 2 How do I write natural-sounding Spanish?

 3 How do I use the right style?

Look at the sample student answers on the next page.

On this page you can read sample answers to the exam-style questions on page 17. Have the students made their meaning clear?

1. Read one student's answer to the first question, 'Las redes sociales'. The answer gives two details for each bullet point. Fill in ✐ the details in English in the table below.

> Estimado señor:
>
> Uso WhatsApp para contactar con mis amigos porque es una aplicación muy práctica.
>
> Durante la semana, uso el móvil todos los días. Mando mensajes a mis amigos y a mis padres.
>
> Lo malo del móvil es que puede ser adictivo y es caro.
>
> Este sábado, descargaré música y veré vídeos en el ordenador.
>
> Atentamente,
>
> Alexia Thompson

	Detail 1	Detail 2
how Alexia contacts her friends	uses WhatsApp	
how much and for what Alexia uses her mobile		
possible problems with mobiles		
what Alexia will use her computer for this weekend		

2. Now read this response to the second question, 'La vida de hoy'. Fill in ✐ two details for each bullet point in the table below, in English.

> Hola, Juan.
>
> Me llevo muy bien con un chico de mi clase: se llama Felipe, es divertido y jugamos al fútbol todos los días.
>
> Ayer vi una película americana en la tele y me gustó porque los actores eran muy buenos.
>
> La música es mi pasión. Mis amigos y yo siempre descargamos y compartimos las canciones nuevas.
>
> Este fin de semana voy a hablar con mis amigos españoles por Skype y después vamos a compartir fotos del viaje que hicimos hace dos semanas.
>
> Hasta luego,
>
> Toby

	Detail 1	Detail 2
Toby's best friend	Felipe	
Toby's favourite TV programme last week		
importance of music		
how Toby will use social networks this weekend		

How do I write clear sentences in Spanish?

To make your meaning clear, you need to pay attention to detail by:

- checking that verbs agree with the subject
- making adjectives agree with the nouns they describe
- checking that noun genders are accurate and using the correct articles: *el, la, los, las.*

① Read the paragraph and circle Ⓐ the correct verb form in each sentence.

> *Mis aplicaciones preferidas [ser / es / son] Instagram y WhatsApp. También [uso / usa / usan]*
> *Facebook de vez en cuando. A mi amiga, Gemma, le encanta Facebook y [publico / publicas /*
> *publica] mensajes y fotos nuevas todos los días. Lo malo de la tecnología móvil [soy / es / son] que*
> *cuando el móvil no [funciona / funcionan / funcionar], ¡es un desastre!*

② Knowing the correct gender of each noun helps you to be accurate when using adjectives. Draw lines ✏️ to match the following nouns with the correct adjectives.

A un chico	**a** americana
B una película	**b** buenos
C los actores	**c** nuevas
D las canciones	**d** divertido

③ Fill in the gaps ✏️ in the text below with the correct article: *el, la, los* or *las.*

> *WhatsApp es .... aplicación más económica y más práctica para mandar mensajes a*
> *........................... amigos. Y como siempre tienes .... móvil contigo, siempre*
> *estás en contacto. Pero para escribir emails, ver vídeos y subir .... fotos de las*
> *vacaciones, es más cómodo usar .... ordenador.*

Don't forget:
- nouns referring to females are feminine (*la madre, la hermana, la abuela*)
- nouns referring to males are masculine (*el padre, el tío, el primo*)
- nouns ending in *-a* and *-ión* are usually feminine (*la película, la televisión*), but there are exceptions (*el programa, el idioma*)
- nouns ending in *-o* are usually masculine (*el periódico*), but there are exceptions (*la radio, la foto*).

Learn nouns with their gender and with the correct article: *el móvil, el ordenador, la aplicación, la ventaja.*

2 How do I write natural-sounding Spanish?

You will notice that English and Spanish sentences don't translate word for word. The ideas are the same, but they are expressed in slightly different ways.

Learn to recognise the differences so that you write correct and natural-sounding sentences.

① The following sentences in Spanish contain examples of how Spanish and English express the same ideas in different ways.

a Draw lines 🖉 to link each idea in English to the corresponding example in Spanish. One has been done for you.

b Then translate 🖉 the examples into English in the 'translation' column.

c Use the 'comments' column to explain 🖉 the differences between the Spanish and English way of expressing the same idea.

idea	example	translation	comments
playing a sport	Tengo 15 años.		
age	Hace buen tiempo.		
how long ago	Mi red social preferida es Facebook.		
expressing likes	Jugamos al fútbol todos los días.		
word order	Fuimos a Barcelona hace dos semanas.	We went to Barcelona two weeks ago.	Spanish uses 'hace' plus a time expression, 'dos semanas'. English uses a time expression, 'two weeks', before 'ago'.
watching TV, a film	Me gusta compartir fotos en Instagram.		
weather	Veo vídeos en YouTube.		

Learning vocabulary in complete phrases rather than as separate words will help you.

3 How do I use the right style?

In the exam, you have to use the formal style for the shorter writing task and the informal style for the longer writing task. This is because of who you are writing to.

In Spanish, you talk to your family and friends using *tú* for 'you' and the second person singular of verbs. You address adults and people you don't know using *usted* for 'you' and the same verb form as for 'he/she/it'. The main differences between formal and informal styles are:
- the use of *usted* instead of *tú*
- the use of different verb forms
- the use of *su* and *sus* to mean 'your' with *usted*
- the use of *tu* and *tus* to mean 'your' with *tú*.

(1) You will need to adapt your writing style to the type of task you are doing. Make sure you can recognise and use both informal and formal language. Look at the terms in the box below.

  a Circle Ⓐ the informal terms.

  b Underline Ⓐ the formal terms.

  c Draw lines 🖉 to link each informal term with its formal equivalent.

<u>Estimado señor</u>	¿te gusta?	Hasta luego	la televisión	¿le gusta?
usted	el instituto	la tele	(Hola)	guay	tus profes
tú	magnífico	Atentamente	sus profesores	el insti

(2) Read the sentences **a**–**e** below and compare the words in italics with the ones in the box below. Choose a word or phrase from the box to replace the words in italics. Then rewrite 🖉 the sentences as if you were writing to a friend.

¡Qué guay!	flipante	superbien	¡Qué rollo!	me molan

  a Me llevo *muy bien* con mi amiga, Julia. *Me llevo superbien con mi amiga, Julia.*

  b Estoy haciendo un ejercicio de matemáticas. *Es bastante complicado.*

  ....

  c Iremos de viaje a Sevilla en junio. *Será muy interesante.*

  ....

  d Me gusta mucho leer y *me encantan* las historias de vampiros.

  ....

  e Fuimos a un partido en el Nou Camp y Messi marcó dos goles. ¡Fue *magnífico*!

  ....

(3) Generally, the formal language you will see in the exam appears in the task instructions. Check that you understand what you are being asked to do in these instructions and write them 🖉 in English.

  a qué le gusta comer ....

  b qué idiomas habla ....

  c cuándo va a viajar ....

  d cuál es su película favorita ....

Sample response

To make your meaning clear, you need to:

- write clear sentences
- write natural-sounding Spanish
- use the right style.

Exam-style question

Los libros y la lectura

Usted va a participar en una encuesta de una librería sobre los libros y la lectura. Escriba a la librería para dar sus opiniones sobre:

- qué le gusta leer
- cuándo lee
- si prefiere leer e-books o libros en papel
- qué leerá durante las próximas vacaciones.

Escriba aproximadamente 40–50 palabras **en español**.   (16 marks)

Estimado señor

[Me gusta / Me gusto] ☐ leer revistas y las biografías de deportistas porque me interesa el deporte. Leo los fines de semana y durante [los / las] ☐ vacaciones. Prefiero [leo / leer] ☐ e-books porque son más [transportable / transportables] ☐ que [el / los] ☐ libros en papel. Durante las próximas vacaciones [leeré / leo] ☐ la biografía del atleta español Kilian Jornet.

[Atentamente / Hasta luego] ☐

Maya Warren

---

(1) Look at the pairs of words written in brackets in the sample answer above.

  (a) Cross out (X) the incorrect word in each case.

  (b) Identify the type of correction by writing (✎): V (verb), A (article), ADJ (adjective), R (register: formal/informal) in each answer box.

Exam-style question

Un mensaje en WhatsApp

Tu amigo, Andrés, te mandó un mensaje esta mañana y quiere saber qué estás haciendo.

Escribe un respuesta a Andrés.

Debes incluir los puntos siguientes:

- qué estás haciendo ahora
- qué hiciste ayer
- qué tiempo hace
- qué vas a hacer mañana.

Escribe aproximadamente 80–90 palabras **en español**.   (20 marks)

Hola, Andrés.

Ahora mismo estoy viendo una peli en casa con mi hermano mayor. Es una película bastante vieja, pero es muy divertida. Ayer jugué al fútbol por la mañana y por la tarde preparamos una cena especial para celebrar el cumpleaños de mi madre. Te mando una foto del pastel que hicimos. ¡Estaba buenísimo! Quiero salir en bici, pero no puedo porque hace mal tiempo: está lloviendo mucho. Creo que mañana vamos a dar una vuelta por el parque o vamos a ir de excursión al campo. Hasta luego.

Robbie

---

(2) Now look at the sample answer to the second exam-style question. Note (✎) on paper examples of the following ways of writing in an informal style:

  (a) opening greeting
  (b) two informal vocabulary items
  (c) informal 'you' form
  (d) closing the message

Your turn!

You are now going to plan and write your response to one of these exam-style tasks from page 17.

Exam-style question

Las redes sociales

Una página web para jóvenes busca su opinión sobre los usos del móvil y del ordenador.

Escriba usted a la página web con la información siguiente:

Exam-style question

La vida de hoy

Juan, tu amigo español, te pregunta sobre tu vida.

Escribe un email para contestarle.

1. First, jot down ✎ your ideas using language you know you can write in Spanish.

Las redes sociales
- how you keep in touch with friends
  ....
- how much you use your mobile each week
  ....
- problems of using mobiles
  ....
- what you will use your computer for this weekend
  ....

La vida de hoy
- a special friend
  ....
- the TV programmes you liked best last week and why
  ....
- what music means to you
  ....
- how you're going to use social networks this weekend
  ....

2. Write ✎ your answer to one of the questions above. Then check your work with the checklist.

....
....
....
....
....
....
....
....
....
....
....

Checklist In my answers do I ...	✓
answer all the bullet points?	
use the correct form of the verbs to match the subjects?	
use the correct articles and adjectives to match the noun genders?	
identify where things are said differently in Spanish and English?	
use the right style ('register') – formal for writing to someone I don't know, informal for writing to a friend?	

Review your skills

Check up

Review your response to the exam-style question on page 23. Tick ✓ the column to show how well you think you have done each of the following.

	Not quite ✓	Nearly there ✓	Got it! ✓
written clear sentences	☐	☐	☐
written natural-sounding Spanish	☐	☐	☐
used the right style	☐	☐	☐

Need more practice?

On paper, plan and write 🖉 your response to the tasks below.

Exam-style question

Las relaciones con la familia y los amigos

Usted participa en una encuesta en línea sobre la familia y los amigos.

Escriba a esta página web con la información siguiente:

- cómo es su familia
- si se lleva bien con toda su familia
- cómo es su mejor amigo o amiga
- qué hará con los amigos durante las próximas vacaciones.

Escriba aproximadamente 40–50 palabras **en español**.

To write a good answer, remember to:
- deal with all four bullet points
- use verb forms and tenses accurately
- use the correct style and register.

(16 marks)

Exam-style question

Un informe sobre la tecnología móvil

Tu amiga española, Elisabet, te hace preguntas para un informe que va a escribir sobre los usos de la tecnología móvil.

Escríbele una respuesta.

Debes incluir los puntos siguientes:

- qué aplicaciones usan más tus amigos
- qué tipo de tecnología móvil usaste más la semana pasada para contactar con tus amigos
- qué tipo de tecnología móvil usan tus padres y tus abuelos
- si vas a ver películas o vídeos en la tele o en el ordenador esta noche.

Escribe aproximadamente 80–90 palabras **en español**.

(20 marks)

How confident do you feel about each of these **skills**? Colour in 🖉 the bars.

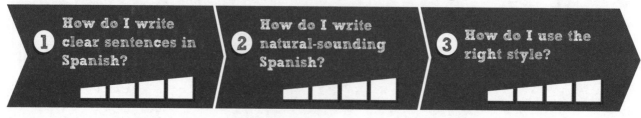

1 How do I write clear sentences in Spanish?

2 How do I write natural-sounding Spanish?

3 How do I use the right style?

④ Writing effectively about the past

This unit will help you learn how to write effectively about the past. The skills you will build are to:

- use opportunities to write about the past
- vary references to the past to add interest
- use past-tense verbs correctly.

In the exam, you will be asked to tackle writing tasks such as the one below. As part of this task, you have to write in the present tense and also refer to the future and the past. This unit will prepare you to write your own response to this question, focusing on the parts that require you to write about the past.

Exam-style question

El deporte y el tiempo libre

Tu amiga española, Luisa, te pregunta sobre tu tiempo libre.

Escríbele un email.

Debes incluir los puntos siguientes:

- tus deportes preferidos
- el deportista que más admiras y por qué
- un fin de semana reciente
- tus ideas para seguir activo/a en el futuro.

Escribe aproximadamente 80–90 palabras **en español**.

(20 marks)

The three key questions in the **skills boosts** will help you to improve how you write about the past.

 1 How do I use opportunities to write about the past?

 2 How do I vary references to the past for added interest?

 3 How do I make sure I use the past tense correctly?

Look at the sample student answer on the next page.

1 Read one student's answer to the task on page 25 and answer 🖉 the questions that follow it, in English.

> **Exam-style question**
>
> **El deporte y el tiempo libre**
> Tu amiga española, Luisa, te pregunta sobre tu tiempo libre.
> Escríbele un email.

Me encanta el deporte y soy una persona bastante activa. Ayer, por ejemplo, jugué al baloncesto en el insti y por la tarde, jugué al hockey. También me gusta nadar y correr, y juego al tenis los martes.

El deportista que más admiro es Rafael Nadal porque juega muy bien y porque ha ganado muchos campeonatos.

El sábado pasado, salí en bici por la mañana, luego nadé y después hice gimnasia. Por la tarde, fui de compras con mis padres. ¡El domingo no hice nada!

El año que viene, quiero participar en un mini-triatlón, por eso voy a correr más.

Leila

---

a How does Leila describe herself?

....

b What sports does she do?

....

c Which sportsperson does she mention and why?

....

d What did she do last Saturday?

....

e What did she do on Sunday?

....

f Which two future plans does she mention?

....

2 Read Leila's answer again. List 🖉 the following, in Spanish:

a examples of one past, one present and one future time phrase:

past: .... present: .... future: ....

b one verb that describes what Rafael Nadal has done (perfect tense):

....

c four verbs Leila uses to say what she did last weekend (preterite tense):

....

d a verb phrase expressing the near future: ....

① How do I use opportunities to write about the past?

Make sure you respond appropriately to a question that refers to the past. If you want to you can add more references to the past when covering other bullets, but you don't have to. Varying the tenses you use will make your writing more interesting and more informative.

① Make sure you identify the bullet points that **require** you to write in the past. Tick ✓ the bullet points in this list that refer to the past.

- **a** la última vez que fuiste al cine
- **b** la mejor canción del año pasado
- **c** una serie de televisión que nunca te pierdes
- **d** tus planes para el verano
- **e** un libro que te gustó
- **f** la persona a quien más admiras

When you're writing about what you usually do, you can add interest and information by referring to past events and experiences too. For example, look at Leila's answer from page 26:

> Me encanta el deporte y soy una persona bastante activa. Ayer, por ejemplo, jugué al baloncesto en el insti y por la tarde, jugué al hockey.

② Now read these answers to the question: *¿Qué sueles hacer en tu tiempo libre?*
Draw lines ✏ to pair up sentences **A–D** with sentences **a–d** so they make sense.

A Los sábados por la mañana, toco la guitarra y mi hermana toca la batería.	a Sin embargo, ayer salimos al parque a correr.
B En mi familia, no somos muy deportistas.	b Pero el domingo pasado, vi un documental fascinante.
C Mi padre siempre cocina los domingos y yo le ayudo.	c Hace dos semanas, toqué en un concierto en el instituto.
D Generalmente, prefiero ver series policíacas y comedias.	d La semana pasada, hicimos una paella. ¡Estaba riquísima!

③ Look at the time expressions below. Number them ✏ in chronological order, starting in the past and finishing in the future.

ayer	el mes pasado
mañana	el año pasado
hace dos semanas	el mes que viene
la semana pasada	el fin de semana que viene

④ Write ✏ two sentences in Spanish about your free time and include something about the past. Use the time expressions in **③** and the sentences in **②** to help you.
Example: *En mis ratos libres, escucho música y toco el teclado. La semana pasada, vi un concierto de música electrónica en la tele. Fue fantástico.*

2 How do I vary references to the past for added interest?

You can write about the past in different ways. For example, you can:
- contrast what you usually do with something unusual
- comment on what happened to show your opinion
- add detail for interest.

Read what Jorge says about his free time and about a recent weekend.

> Generalmente, los fines de semana me quedo en casa. Veo la tele, escucho música y descanso. Sin embargo, el sábado pasado, salí al parque por la noche con mi familia. Pero no fuimos a pasear, fuimos a ver una película al cine al aire libre. Lo pasé bomba porque la película fue genial y además, hacía buen tiempo. Desafortunadamente, mi padre se durmió y no vio el final de la peli. ¡Por suerte no roncó!

Use a variety of verbs, and refer to other people in your writing, to avoid repetition and to add interest. For example, Jorge writes *salí al parque*, but then he uses the first person plural, *fuimos*, and later refers to his father: *mi padre se durmió*.

① Tick ✓ to say whether these statements about Jorge's text are true or false.

		true	false
a	Jorge usually goes out at the weekend.		
b	Last weekend, he went out with his family.		
c	They went to the cinema in the shopping centre.		
d	Jorge enjoyed the evening.		
e	The film was great.		
f	Jorge missed the end of the film because he fell asleep.		
g	Luckily, Jorge's dad didn't snore.		

② a In Jorge's text, circle Ⓐ four verbs that describe what he usually does.

b Underline Ⓐ three expressions he uses to introduce a contrast.

c Highlight ✐ the sentence that gives Jorge's opinion.

③ On paper, write ✐ a short text saying what you usually do at the weekend and contrasting it with something unusual that happened. Use the words/phrases below and the time expressions on page 27 to help you.

Generalmente Normalmente	Pero Sin embargo	Desafortunadamente Por suerte	Fue genial / estupendo / fatal / un desastre ¡Qué guay! Lo pasé bien / bomba / fenomenal

Checklist In my answer do I ...	✓
say what I usually do at the weekend?	
add detail for interest?	
add something unusual that happened, as a contrast?	
give an opinion about what happened?	

3 How do I make sure I use the past tense correctly?

In Spanish, the preterite tense is used to write about events and completed actions in the past. This means you need to:

- know the correct preterite endings for -ar, -er and -ir verbs
- know the preterite form of irregular verbs and verbs with spelling changes
- use the correct form of the verb in the preterite to match the subject.

Preterite verb endings

Regular verbs		Common irregular verbs			Verbs with spelling changes		
-ar e.g. comprar	-er / -ir e.g. comer	ser / ir	hacer	ver	tocar	jugar	dormir
compré	comí	fui	hice	vi	toqué	jugué	dormí
compraste	comiste	fuiste	hiciste	viste	tocaste	jugaste	dormiste
compró	comió	fue	hizo	vio	tocó	jugó	durmió
compramos	comimos	fuimos	hicimos	vimos	tocamos	jugamos	dormimos
comprasteis	comisteis	fuisteis	hicisteis	visteis	tocasteis	jugasteis	dormisteis
compraron	comieron	fueron	hicieron	vieron	tocaron	jugaron	durmieron

① Read Robert's email to his friend, Alberto, in Spain.

Hola, Alberto.

El fin de semana pasado lo pasé superbién. El viernes por la noche salí con mis amigos. Fuimos a la bolera.

El sábado jugué en un torneo de baloncesto y ganó mi equipo. El domingo fui a la fiesta de cumpleaños

de mi prima. Primero había una cena especial y luego, mis tíos y sus amigos, que antes tocaban en una

banda, se vistieron de* los Rolling Stones y tocaron dos canciones. Te mandaré fotos. ¡Qué risa! Fue genial.

Hasta luego.

*vestirse de – to dress as

Robert

a Underline (A) all the verbs in the preterite tense.

b Now write them (✎) beside their English translations below.

I had a great time: ....

I went out: ....

we went: ....

I played: ....

(the team) won: ....

I went: ....

they dressed as: ....

they played: ....

it was: ....

② Read Alberto's reply to Robert. Fill the gaps (✎) with the correct preterite form of the verbs in brackets.

¡Qué fin de semana más guay! Gracias por las fotos de la fiesta. Pues, yo el fin de sábado pasado,

[ver] .... una película en la tele. Luego [ir] .... al polideportivo y

[jugar] .... al balonmano. Después [salir] .... al parque a pasear al perro,

[tocar] .... la guitarra un rato y [descansar] .... bastante. El domingo

mi hermana [jugar] .... un partido de voleibol y luego [nosotros – ir] ....

todos a comer a casa de mis abuelos.

Sample response

Here is Kieran's answer to the task on page 25. Has he followed all the advice and written effectively about the past?

Exam-style question

- tus deportes preferidos
- el deportista que más admiras y por qué
- un fin de semana reciente
- tus ideas para seguir activo/a en el futuro.

Mi deporte preferido es el rugby y admiro a Billy Vunipola porque es fuerte y valiente. La semana pasada vi un partido estupendo de rugby en la tele.

No soy muy deportista, pero el año pasado gané un campeonato de tenis de mesa en el insti.

Hace poco, pasé el fin de semana cerca de la playa con mi familia. Fue genial porque dormimos en una tienda y cocinamos al aire libre. ¡Además, mis hermanos y yo no nos peleamos!

Creo que en el futuro, vamos a ir más al campo a hacer camping y a caminar.

Kieran

1 Find in the text examples of the things listed below. Note 🖉 them in the table.

use an opportunity to link a past event with the present	Mi deporte preferido es el rugby... vi un partido estupendo
use a time phrase to refer to the past	
use a past event as contrast	
give an opinion about an event in the past	
use the correct preterite endings for regular verbs	
correctly spell preterite verbs that are irregular / have spelling changes	
vary the verb forms (that is, not just using first person singular)	

Your turn!

You are now going to plan and write your own response to the exam-style task on page 25.

the exam-style task on page 25.

Exam-style question

El deporte y el tiempo libre

Tu amiga española, Luisa, te pregunta sobre tu tiempo libre.

Escríbele un email.

(1) First, jot down 🖉 your ideas for each bullet point, in Spanish.

• What sports do you like? ....

   Did you play in a match / watch a sporting event recently? ....

   If you're not keen on sports, what do you prefer doing? ....

• Which sportsperson / other well-known person do you admire most and why? ....

   ....

• What did you do at a weekend recently? ....

   Did you do something you particularly enjoyed? ....

   What was good about it? ....

   Did the weekend include friends and family? If so, what did they do? ....

   ....

• What are your future plans in terms of sport/keeping fit? ....

(2) Answer 🖉 the question. Then check your work with the checklist.

Checklist In my answer do I ...	✓
use a past tense if a bullet point mentions the past?	
use an opportunity to refer to the past?	
use a time phrase to refer to the past, e.g. *la semana pasada?*	
use a word to introduce a contrast, e.g. *pero, sin embargo?*	
give an opinion about something in the past?	
use verbs correctly in the preterite, including both regular and irregular verbs?	
use other persons of the verb, not just the first person singular ('I')?	

Review your skills

Check up

Review your response to the exam-style question on page 31. Tick ✓ the column to show how well you think you have done each of the following.

	Not quite ✓	Nearly there ✓	Got it! ✓
used opportunities to write about the past	☐	☐	☐
varied references to the past to add interest	☐	☐	☐
used the preterite tense correctly	☐	☐	☐

Need more practice?

On paper, plan and write ✐ your response to the exam-style task below.

Exam-style question

El tiempo libre, tus intereses y tú

Con tu clase, vas a ir a España en un intercambio. Tienes que contestar las preguntas de un cuestionario para encontrar una familia compatible.

Debes incluir los puntos siguientes:

- qué te gusta hacer cuando estás en casa
- tus pasatiempos favoritos
- si fuiste recientemente al cine, al teatro o a un concierto que te gustó
- tus planes para el fin de semana que viene.

Escribe aproximadamente 80–90 palabras **en español**.

(20 marks)

To write a good answer, try to include:

- reference to past, present and future events
- sentences that are linked together
- a variety of structures and vocabulary
- a personal opinion.

How confident do you feel about each of these **skills**? Colour in ✐ the bars.

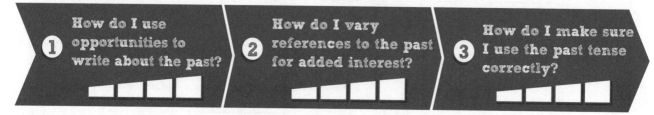

1 How do I use opportunities to write about the past?

2 How do I vary references to the past for added interest?

3 How do I make sure I use the past tense correctly?

⑤ Writing effectively about the future

This unit will help you learn how to use the future tense successfully. The skills you will build are to:

- use opportunities to write about the future
- use the future tense correctly
- vary references to the future for added interest.

In the exam, you will be asked to tackle writing tasks such as the two below. This unit will prepare you to plan and write your own responses to these questions.

Exam-style question

Una semana en mi ciudad

Tu clase propone hacer un intercambio con una clase en un instituto español.

Escriba un email a la profesora española y cuéntele lo siguiente:

- cómo es la ciudad
- qué hay para hacer
- lo mejor de la ciudad
- qué hará durante la visita.

Escriba aproximadamente 40–50 palabras **en español**.

(16 marks)

Exam-style question

Mi área local

Tu amiga Berta se interesa por la zona donde vives.

Escríbele una respuesta.

Debes incluir los puntos siguientes:

- dónde está situado/a tu pueblo/ciudad
- el clima de tu zona
- un sitio de interés que visitaste recientemente
- posibles actividades para el próximo fin de semana.

Escribe aproximadamente 80–90 palabras **en español**.

(20 marks)

Each question has one bullet point that asks you to write about something in the future.
The three key questions in the **skills boosts** will help you write effectively about the future.

1 How do I use opportunities to write about the future?

2 How do I use the future tense correctly?

3 How do I vary references to the future for added interest?

Look at the sample student answers on the next page.

1 Read the bullet points of the second exam-style question on page 33 and write 🖊 what tense you have to use in each case. Use 'P' for present, 'Pret' for preterite and 'F' for future.

Exam-style question

- dónde está situado/a tu pueblo/ciudad

- el clima de tu zona

- un sitio de interés que visitaste recientemente

- posibles actividades para el próximo fin de semana

2 Read one student's answer to the second writing task on page 33 and answer 🖊 the questions that follow it, in English.

> Mi pueblo está situado al lado del mar y está rodeado de montañas. Tiene unas vistas muy bonitas.
>
> El clima es variable, hace sol, pero también llueve a menudo. En invierno hace bastante frío y viento.
>
> Hace dos semanas visité un castillo que está en el centro del pueblo; creo que es lo mejor de este lugar, además del paisaje. El próximo fin de semana, si hace buen tiempo, mis amigos y yo iremos a la costa y descansaremos en la playa. ¡Será guay!

a Where is the town situated? ....

....

b What has the town got to offer? ....

....

c What's the weather like in winter? ....

....

d When did the student visit the castle? ....

....

e What did the student think of the castle? ....

....

f What will the friends do at the beach? ....

....

3 Read the sample answer again and highlight 🖊 the different tenses the student uses, using a different colour for each tense.

1 How do I use opportunities to write about the future?

Make sure you respond appropriately to a question that refers to the future. If you want to, you can add more references to the future when covering other bullet points, but you don't have to.

(1) First, make sure you identify the bullet points that **require** you to write about the future. Tick ✓ the bullet points in this list that refer to the future.

a lo qué se puede hacer en tu zona

b lo qué harás en tu pueblo el sábado que viene

c lo qué hiciste ayer por la noche

d dónde irás si hace buen tiempo

e lo mejor de donde vives

f los planes que tienes para este fin de semana

(2) Read four responses to this bullet point: *menciona lo mejor de tu región*. Sentences **A–D** below say something about **what there is to do** in the student's region. Sentences **a–d** add something **they will do**. Draw lines 🖉 to pair them up so they make sense.

A Aquí tenemos una costa muy bonita.	**a** El mes que viene mi familia y yo practicaremos senderismo en el campo.
B En mi región se puede disfrutar de paisajes impresionantes.	**b** En el verano haré windsurf y practicaré otros deportes al aire libre. ¡Qué guay!
C Lo mejor de mi región es el río cerca de donde vivo.	**c** El fin de semana que viene iremos a la playa. Me gustará mucho.
D En Cornwall se puede gozar del buen tiempo.	**d** Durante las vacaciones iré de excursión en barco por el río. ¡Será superdivertido!

(3) Read sentences **a–d** in **(2)** again and underline Ⓐ the time phrases that introduce a reference to the future.

(4) Here are other time phrases you may recognise. Match 🖉 the Spanish phrases with their English equivalents.

A la semana que viene	**a** tonight
B esta noche	**b** next Saturday
C el sábado que viene	**c** the day after tomorrow
D pasado mañana	**d** next week

(5) On paper, invent other endings for sentences **a–d** in **(2)**, using phrases on this page and others you know.

(6) On paper, write 🖉 your own answer to the bullet point in **(2)**: *menciona lo mejor de tu región*. You can use the same verbs.

2 **How do I use the future tense correctly?**

To use the future tense correctly, make sure you:
- know all the correct verb endings
- learn common irregular verbs, such as *hacer – haré*.

Remember that, in the **future tense**, *-ar*, *-er* and *-ir* verbs all have the same endings:

Hablar

hablar**é**
hablar**ás**
hablar**á**
hablar**emos**
hablar**éis**
hablar**án**

Some verbs have irregular stems in the future tense, but the endings are the same as for regular verbs. These include:

hacer	**har-**	*to make, do*
poner	**pondr-**	*to put, place, set*
salir	**saldr-**	*to leave, go out*
tener	**tendr-**	*to have*
venir	**vendr-**	*to come*

① Read this email written to a Spanish friend, in which the writer gives details of the weekend they are going to spend in the countryside. Fill the gaps 🖊 with the correct form of the verb given in brackets.

> *¡Hola!*
>
> *Este fin de semana [hacer] .... camping con mi familia en la sierra cerca de mi*
>
> *ciudad. [disfrutar] .... de paisajes impresionantes y mis padres y yo [practicar]*
>
> *.................................... senderismo. Si hace calor, [nosotros – nadar] ....*
>
> *en los lagos y mi madre [leer] .... una novela al sol. Mi padre [preparar]*
>
> *.................................... la comida y [nosotros – comer] .... al aire libre. El domingo*
>
> *[nosotros – ir] .... de excursión y [nosotros – visitar] .... unas*
>
> *cuevas con estalagmitas*. ¡[3rd person – ser] .... flipante!*

*stalagmites

② This answer about a future school trip has **nine** mistakes in the verb forms.

a Find and circle Ⓐ them.

> *El mes que viene yo (fue) a Madrid con mi clase. Nos alojar en una pensión por cinco noches.*
> *Visitaron el museo del Prado y el Parque del Retiro. Lo mejor son la visita guiada al Estadio*
> *Bernabeu porque me mola el fútbol. El domingo por la mañana mis compañeros y yo irá al mercado*
> *del Rastro y yo compré recuerdos. Una tarde nosotros salir a una churrería y comer churros con*
> *chocolate. ¡Qué rico! La visita son superdivertida.*

b Write 🖊 the correct verb forms in the answer spaces below.

i ....   iv ....   vii ....

ii ....   v ....   viii ....

iii ....   vi ....   ix ....

③ Now imagine you are going on a school trip. On paper, write 🖊 an email to describe what you will do (about 50 words). Try to include different persons of the verb, such as *(nosotros) comeremos*. Make sure you use the future tense correctly!

3 How do I vary references to the future for added interest?

Giving an example of what you are planning to do is one way to introduce the future, but there are others. For instance:

- say what you're going to do **if something happens**
- say what you're going to do **according to the weather**.

And remember, you don't have to refer to yourself all the time. You can also describe what other people will do.

1 Read this email to a Spanish friend about plans for the weekend.

> Este sábado por la mañana, <u>si hace buen tiempo, jugaré al fútbol</u> en el parque con mis amigos. Pero si llueve, cogeremos el autobús al centro comercial. Compraré un regalo para mi madre porque es su cumpleaños y después si tenemos hambre, comeremos una hamburguesa. Por la tarde, si viene mi primo a mi casa, iremos a la bolera y por la noche veremos un box set. ¡Será divertido! El domingo haré los deberes y si termino pronto, mi hermano y yo iremos a la pista de hielo.

> Use 'if' clauses to discuss possible plans for the future and what you will do depending on the weather:
> Si + **present**, + future
> Si **hace** sol, **iremos** a la costa.
> If it's sunny, we will go to the coast.
> Si **tengo** tiempo, **visitaré** el castillo.
> If I have time, I will visit the castle.

a Underline (A) all the *si* + present, + future phrases.

b Then translate those phrases into English.

Example: *si hace buen tiempo, jugaré al fútbol*: if the weather is good, I will play football

....

....

....

....

2 **a** Complete the sentences below with suitable *Si* + **present tense** phrases.

...., iré a la playa y nadaré en el mar.

...., visitaré el museo.

...., compraré unas zapatillas de deporte nuevas.

b Now complete these sentences with phrases using the **future tense**. Look at **1** to help you.

Si hace buen tiempo, yo ....

Si llueve, mis amigos y yo ....

Si tenemos tiempo, mi familia y yo ....

3 Now it's your turn. Make up full sentences about possible activities using *Si* + **present**, + **future**.

....

....

....

....

....

Sample response

Look again at the exam-style writing tasks on page 33 ('Una semana en mi ciudad' and 'Mi área local'). Now look at two students' answers to the questions. Do they write effectively about the future?

A

La ciudad es bastante grande y hay mucho que hacer, por ejemplo se puede visitar los museos y la catedral. Lo mejor es que hay una pista de hielo estupenda. Haremos muchas cosas, por ejemplo iremos en autocar a un parque temático y si hace buen tiempo, haremos una excursión al campo. ¡Será fantástico!

B

Mi pueblo está al norte del país, al lado de un río. Es un pueblo muy antiguo y bonito. Hace mucho calor en verano, sin embargo, en invierno a veces nieva. El fin de semana pasado hice una excursión en barco por el río, ¡fue impresionante! El próximo fin de semana, mis amigos y yo visitaremos un pueblo en la costa y haremos deportes acuáticos, por ejemplo, si hace viento, practicaré el windsurf. Después compraremos patatas fritas y las comeremos en la playa y si tengo bastante dinero, compraré un helado también. ¡Lo pasaré bien!

(1) Read the students' answers again and try to find at least one example of each of the things listed below. Note 🖉 them in the table, in Spanish.

	A	B
time phrases to indicate the future		El próximo fin de semana
something that the writer is planning to do		
a variety of verbs in the future tense		
any irregular verbs in the future tense		
verbs referring to persons other than 'yo'		
using the weather to talk about the future		
si + present, + future		

Your turn!

You are now going to plan and write your response to both the exam-style tasks from page 33.

from page 33

Exam-style question

Una semana en mi ciudad

Tu clase propone hacer un intercambio con una clase en un instituto español.

Escriba un email a la profesora española...

Exam-style question

Mi área local

Tu amiga Berta se interesa por la zona donde vives.

Escríbele una respuesta.

(1) First jot down 🖉 your ideas for each bullet point.

Una semana en mi ciudad

• What is your town like?

....

• What is there to do?

....

• What is the best thing about your town?

....

• What activities are you planning to do during the visit?

....

Mi área local

• Where is the town?

....

• What is the weather like in your region?

....

• Where did you visit recently?

....

• What possible activities could you do in your area next weekend?

....

(2) Write 🖉 your answer to one of the questions above. Then check your work with the checklist.

....

....

....

....

....

....

....

....

....

....

....

....

Checklist In my answer do I ...	A ✓	B ✓
use time phrases to indicate the future?		
give examples of something I am planning to do?		
use a variety of verbs in the future tense?		
use any irregular verbs in the future tense?		
use verbs referring to persons other than *yo*?		
use the weather to talk about the future?		
use *si* + present tense, + future tense?		

Review your skills

Check up

Review your response to the exam-style questions on page 33. Tick ✓ the column to show how well you think you have done each of the following.

	Not quite ✓	Nearly there ✓	Got it! ✓
used opportunities to write about the future	☐	☐	☐
used the future tense correctly	☐	☐	☐
varied references to the future for added interest	☐	☐	☐

Need more practice?

On paper, plan and write ✐ your response to the exam-style tasks below.

Exam-style question

Los pros y contras de mi ciudad

Usted quiere informar a un compañero de trabajo sobre lo mejor y lo peor de su ciudad.

Escriba usted un email y cuéntele lo siguiente:

- qué hay en tu zona
- lo mejor de tu ciudad
- lo peor de tu ciudad
- dónde irá el fin de semana próximo.

Escriba aproximadamente 40–50 palabras **en español**. (16 marks)

Exam-style question

¿Cómo es tu ciudad?

Tu amigo español quiere saber algo de tu ciudad y te escribe un correo.

Escríbele una respuesta.

Debes incluir los puntos siguientes:

- la zona donde vives
- lo que puedes hacer
- algo divertido que hiciste en tu ciudad recientemente
- los planes que tienes para participar en una futura actividad.

Escribe aproximadamente 80–90 palabras **en español**. (20 marks)

To write a good answer, try to include:
- relevant information, some with extra details
- as little repetition as possible
- references to the future using the future tense.

How confident do you feel about each of these **skills**? Colour in ✐ the bars.

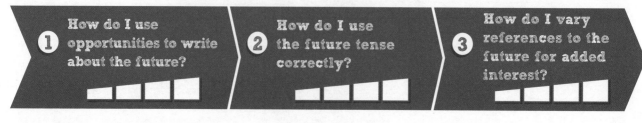

1 How do I use opportunities to write about the future?

2 How do I use the future tense correctly?

3 How do I vary references to the future for added interest?

⑥ Choosing and linking your ideas

This unit will help you learn how to choose and link your ideas in your written answers. The skills you will build are to help you:

- choose what you want to say
- organise your answer
- link your ideas logically.

In the exam, you will be asked to tackle writing tasks such as the one below. This unit will prepare you to write your own response to this question.

Exam-style question

Navidad en España

Tu amiga española, Elena, te envió un email sobre las fiestas en Inglaterra.

Escríbele una respuesta.

Debes incluir los puntos siguientes:

- cómo se celebra el Año Nuevo en tu pueblo o ciudad
- cuáles fueron los días más importantes durante las vacaciones de Navidad
- las celebraciones en tu familia durante el año
- los planes que tienes para ver las fiestas en España.

Escribe aproximadamente 80–90 palabras **en español**.   (20 marks)

The three key questions in the **skills boosts** will help you to produce a structured response.

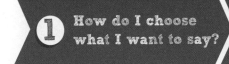 **1** How do I choose what I want to say? **2** How do I organise my answer? **3** How do I link my ideas logically?

Look at the sample student answer on the next page.

Look again at the exam-style question from page 41, then read the sample student answer that follows.

Exam-style question

Navidad en España

Tu amiga española, Elena, te envió un email sobre las fiestas en Inglaterra.

Escríbele una respuesta.

Debes incluir los puntos siguientes:

- cómo se celebra el Año Nuevo en tu pueblo o ciudad
- cuáles fueron los días más importantes durante las vacaciones de Navidad
- las celebraciones en tu familia durante el año
- los planes que tienes para ver las fiestas en España.

Escribe aproximadamente 80–90 palabras **en español**.   (20 marks)

En mi pueblo normalmente celebramos Año Nuevo con una fiesta. Me gusta mucho porque bailamos y cantamos. En el pueblo también organizamos fuegos artificiales.

El día de Navidad fue especial porque recibimos muchos regalos, pero lo mejor fue la Nochevieja. Por la noche preparamos una comida de celebración.

En casa cuando celebramos un cumpleaños, por ejemplo, invitamos a toda la familia. ¡Lo pasamos bomba!

Me encantan estas fiestas y además me gustaría ver las celebraciones en otro país. El año próximo voy a ir a la Feria de Abril en Sevilla. Creo que será bonito.

(1) How well has the writer addressed the four bullet points? Fill in 🖉 the table in English.

	Fact(s)	Example(s)	Opinion(s)	Reason(s)
• Año Nuevo	party	–	likes it a lot	dances and sings
• días más importantes				
• celebraciones durante el año				
• planes para ver fiestas				

(2) Read the student's text again. How did they link their ideas? Note down 🖉 which words they have used to:

(a) give the reason why they like the New Year celebrations. .....porque.....................

(b) say what else the town does to celebrate New Year. ....

(c) explain why Christmas Day is special. ....

(d) introduce the opinion that Christmas Eve was the best day. ....

(e) introduce the example of a family birthday. ....

(f) say they would like to see festivals being celebrated in other countries. ....

(g) give their opinion about the Feria. ....

How do I choose what I want to say?

Your starting point is the list of bullet points in the task: you need to make sure you deal with every one of them. Make sure you respond using the right content, tenses and vocabulary.

Look again at each of the four bullet points from the exam-style question on page 41:

Exam style question

- cómo se celebra el Año Nuevo en tu pueblo o ciudad
- cuáles fueron los días más importantes durante las vacaciones de Navidad
- las celebraciones en tu familia durante el año
- los planes que tienes para ver las fiestas en España.

① Read the facts that one student has jotted down as notes for each bullet point. In each case, one of the facts is not relevant. Mark a cross ⊗ against the irrelevant fact.

• *hace un mes*	*por la noche*	*normalmente*
• *Semana Santa*	*Año Nuevo*	*Nochevieja*
• *ir al instituto*	*fuegos artificiales*	*comida con familia*
• *ver celebraciones diferentes*	*tener una experiencia nueva*	*tomar el sol en la playa*

② ⓐ Which tenses will you use when responding to bullet points **a–d**? Write ✎ the relevant tense (present, past or future) in the table below.

ⓑ What is the content of your response going to be? Complete ✎ the table in Spanish for each of the bullet points.

> Remember that regular -ar and -ir verbs have the same 'we' form for both past and present; -er verbs only change one vowel.

Bullet point	Tense	Notes
i Año Nuevo		
ii días más importantes		
iii celebraciones durante el año	*present*	
iv planes para ver fiestas		

③ Choose verb forms for each bullet point wisely. Select the ones you are most confident about. Look at the 'we' verb forms below. Match ✎ the Spanish verbs with their English meanings.

A celebramos	a we danced
B bailamos	b we sang
C cantamos	c we received
D recibimos	d we prepared
E preparamos	e we had (a good time)
F lo pasamos (bomba)	f we celebrated

② How do I organise my answer?

Your ideas need to be well chosen but also clearly and sensibly organised. You need to:
- organise your answer in paragraphs corresponding to each bullet point: one paragraph per bullet point
- keep all the ideas addressing the same bullet point together.

① Read the following two-part question and the response underneath. It contains good sentences, but they are not very well organised.

- ¿Qué hiciste para celebrar tu cumpleaños?
- ¿Qué vas a hacer para celebrar tu próximo cumpleaños?

[1] Mi familia y yo fuimos a un restaurante italiano para celebrar mi cumpleaños. [2] El año que viene me gustaría hacer una fiesta en casa. [3] Lo pasé bien pero el servicio era lento. [4] Voy a invitar a mis amigos. [5] El helado es mi postre favorito y la tarta helada estaba deliciosa. [6] Bailaremos y cantaremos. [7] ¡Será superdivertido! [8] Lo mejor fue el postre.

ⓐ Sort out the numbered sentences above: which question part do they relate to? Write ✐ the numbers in the boxes.

- ¿Qué hiciste para celebrar tu cumpleaños?

- ¿Qué vas a hacer para celebrar tu próximo cumpleaños?

ⓑ Now organise the sentences into a logical order. Write ✐ the numbers in the right order in the boxes.

② Read the two-part question below and the student notes on the left and right.

Organise the notes: draw lines ✐ to link each note to the right question.

fiesta en España		ropa típica
bandas favoritas	• ¿Cómo fue el festival de música?	demasiado calor
entradas baratas	• ¿Qué planes tienes para el verano que viene?	bailar en las calles
desfiles bonitos		acampar

③ Choose one of the two-part questions from either ① or ② and write ✐ your own notes on paper. Use ② to help you organise them.

3 How do I link my ideas logically?

- Aim for extended sentences that link your ideas, but write logically using the right connectives.
- Develop your use of connectives to help you: build on the basic ones you have already met.

① Match up 🖉 the Spanish connectives with the English meanings.

A además	**a** however
B sobre todo	**b** for this reason
C por eso	**c** in addition
D sin embargo	**d** above all
E también	**e** as
F por un lado	**f** therefore
G tampoco	**g** on the one hand
H así que	**h** on the other hand
I ya que	**i** neither
J por otro lado	**j** also

② Read the following response to these two bullet points:
- ¿Cómo celebras tu cumpleaños normalmente?
- ¿Qué planes tienes para tu próximo cumpleaños?

Fill the gaps 🖉 with appropriate connectives to complete the text, choosing from the options in brackets.

Generalmente celebro mi cumpleaños con mi familia. Lo paso bien [también / porque] ....
recibo regalos y tarjetas y [además / por eso] .... porque mi hermana me hace una tarta
riquísima. [Ya que / Sin embargo], ... el año que viene quiero hacer algo diferente.

Mi cumpleaños es en verano; [por eso / por otro lado] .... voy a ir a un festival de música
con mi mejor amiga. Lo pasaré bien [sobre todo / ya que] .... porque veré a mis grupos
favoritos. Haremos camping y [por un lado / así que] .... el ambiente será increíble, pero
[por lo tanto / por otro lado] .... no dormiré nada [tampoco / ya que] ....
el camping será muy ruidoso.

③ Improve these sentences by filling in the gaps 🖉 with a connective from ①.

a Me gusta la fruta; ...., prefiero los dulces.

b María llegará tarde .... hay mucho tráfico.

c No tengo hambre; .... tengo sed.

d Me gustaría probar la paella .... porque me encanta el arroz.

e Quiero ver a mi grupo favorito; .... voy a ir al festival de música.

Sample response

Look again at the exam-style writing task from page 41 and one student's response below.

Exam-style question

Navidad en España

Tu amiga española, Elena, te envió un email sobre las fiestas en Inglaterra.
Escríbele una respuesta.

Debes incluir los puntos siguientes:

- cómo se celebra el Año Nuevo en tu pueblo o ciudad
- cuál fue el día más importante durante las vacaciones de Navidad
- las celebraciones en tu familia durante el año
- los planes que tienes para ver las fiestas en España.

Escribe aproximadamente 80–90 palabras **en español**. (20 marks)

Para celebrar el Año Nuevo en mi pueblo organizamos una fiesta en el ayuntamiento. Preparamos mucha comida y toca una banda. A medianoche vemos los fuegos artificiales en la calle y por eso me acuesto muy tarde.

Abrimos los regalos el día de Navidad y, además de un teléfono nuevo, recibí muchos libros. Fue el mejor día de las vacaciones, sobre todo porque vi a toda mi familia.

Cuando organizamos una fiesta en casa, sobre todo en verano, preparamos una barbacoa. Además, siempre vamos a una piscina, ya que está muy cerca.

El próximo verano voy a ir a España y, si es posible, quiero ver las fiestas en tu pueblo. Sin embargo, no tengo mucho dinero; por eso me gustaría pasar unos días en tu casa.

---

(1) Has the student followed all the advice about how to choose and link their ideas?
Complete 🖉 the last column of the table with ticks or examples from the answer above.

To be successful in getting your message across in your written answers, you need to:
- choose what you want to say
- organise your answer
- link your ideas logically.

		✓ or 🖉 examples from text
all points made are relevant to the bullets	• Año Nuevo	una fiesta
	• días más importantes	
	• celebraciones en familia	
	• planes para ver fiestas	
used paragraphs		✓
kept all ideas addressing the same point together		
linked ideas logically with connectives to...	add a fact	
	give an alternative	
	give an example	
	create a contrast	
	explain	
	add a consequence	
	say 'if'	

Your turn!

You are now going to plan and write your response to the exam-style task from page 41. Look at the question again.

Exam-style question

Navidad en España

Tu amiga española, Elena, te envió un email sobre las fiestas en Inglaterra.

Escríbele una respuesta.

Debes incluir los puntos siguientes:

- cómo se celebra el Año Nuevo en tu pueblo o ciudad
- cuáles fueron los días más importantes durante las vacaciones de Navidad
- las celebraciones en tu familia durante el año
- los planes que tienes para ver las fiestas en España.

Escribe aproximadamente 80–90 palabras **en español**.   **(20 marks)**

(1) First, plan your answer by jotting down 🖉 your ideas. What will you include? For each bullet point note down 🖉 a couple of words to act as a reminder:

- local New Year celebrations: ....

- most important days over Christmas: ....

- family celebrations: ....

- plans for getting to see festivities in Spain: ....

(2) Now write 🖉 your answer. Once you have finished, read it through and check against the Checklist.

Remember!
- Separate your ideas into clear paragraphs.
- Use **FEOR**: Fact, Example, Opinion, Reason (not necessarily in that order).
- **Order your ideas logically within each paragraph.**
- Only use vocabulary you feel confident with.

Checklist In my answer do I ...	✓
only make points relevant to the bullet points?	
use a paragraph for each bullet point?	
organise my answer, keeping all points that deal with the same point together?	
use FEOR: fact, example, opinion, reason?	
link my ideas logically using connectives?	

Review your skills

Check up

Review your response to the exam-style question on page 47. Tick ✓ the column to show how well you think you have done each of the following.

	Not quite ✓	Nearly there ✓	Got it! ✓
chosen what I wanted to say	☐	☐	☐
organised my answer	☐	☐	☐
linked my ideas logically	☐	☐	☐

Need more practice?

On paper, plan and write 🖉 your response to the exam-style task below.

Exam-style question

Un festival de cine internacional

El verano pasado visitaste un festival de cine internacional.

Escribe a tu amigo/a español/a sobre tu experiencia.

Debes incluir los puntos siguientes:

• dónde y cuándo se celebra el festival

• lo que más te gustó del festival

• por qué los festivales son tan populares hoy

• los planes que tienes para asistir a otro festival en el futuro.

Escribe aproximadamente 80–90 palabras **en español**.   (20 marks)

To write a good answer, try to include:
• relevant information with some extra details
• a variety of structures and tenses
• extended sentences well linked together
• original ideas
• a personal opinion.

How confident do you feel about each of these **skills**? Colour in 🖉 the bars.

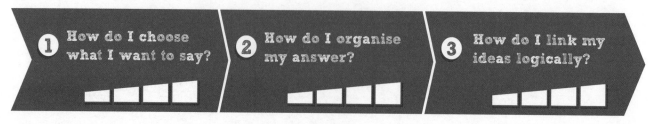

1 How do I choose what I want to say?

2 How do I organise my answer?

3 How do I link my ideas logically?

7 Improving your accuracy

This unit will help you improve your accuracy. The skills you will build are to:

- write correct verb forms
- check agreements
- improve your spelling.

In the exam, you will be asked to tackle writing tasks such as the one below. This unit will prepare you to plan and write your own response to this question, using language that is as accurate as possible.

Exam-style question

El trabajo

Tu amiga española te pregunta sobre el trabajo que tienes los fines de semana.

Escribe una respuesta a tu amiga.

Debes incluir los puntos siguientes:

- en qué consiste tu trabajo y tu horario
- algo interesante que pasó recientemente
- por qué (no) te gusta tu trabajo
- tus planes para el trabajo en el futuro.

Escribe aproximadamente 80–90 palabras **en español**.

(20 marks)

The three key questions in the **skills boosts** will help you to improve your accuracy.

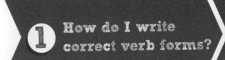
1 How do I write correct verb forms?

2 How do I check agreements?

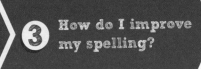
3 How do I improve my spelling?

Look at the sample student answer on the next page.

Read one student's answer to the exam-style question on page 49.

> ¡Hola!
>
> Trabajo los fines de semana en un restaurante de mi barrio. Soy camarera: sirvo comida y bebida a los clientes y a veces ayudo en la cocina. El sábado pasado, tuve que hablar español porque comieron en el restaurante dos señoras argentinas. ¡Vale la pena estudiar idiomas! Me gusta el trabajo porque generalmente los clientes son simpáticos. Lo malo es que tengo poco tiempo libre. El año que viene, voy a hacer un curso de turismo y haré prácticas en un hotel. En el futuro, quiero ser azafata o cocinera.
>
> ¡Hasta pronto!
>
> Amira

(1) What information does Amira give for each bullet point? Write 🖉 notes in English.

- where and when she works now:

  ....

- what she does at work:

  ....

- something that happened recently:

  ....

- why she likes / dislikes the job:

  ....

- her future work plans:

  ....

(2) Now find the following phrases in Amira's text. Write 🖉 them in the spaces in Spanish.

a I work at the weekends

....

b I like the work

....

c I had to speak

....

d They ate in the restaurant

....

e I'm going to do a tourism course

....

f I will do work experience

....

(3) **a** Amira mentions three jobs. Note 🖉 them down in Spanish.

....

b Write 🖉 the names of the same jobs if they referred to a man.

....

c Were the Argentinian customers at the restaurant men or women? Explain 🖉 how you know.

....

....

How do I write correct verb forms?

When you use a verb, ask yourself these questions:
- Am I writing about the past, the present or the future?
- How do I choose the correct tense to write about the past, present or future?

(1) Read the following questions and identify the verbs in them. Then match each question to the appropriate verb tense.

A ¿Ayudas con las tareas en casa?	**a** preterite (for completed events and actions in the past)
B ¿Vas a trabajar durante las vacaciones este verano?	**b** present (for what you do now and what you usually do)
C ¿Qué trabajo quieres hacer en el futuro?	**c** immediate future (*voy a* + infinitive for near future plans)
D ¿Estudiarás idiomas el año que viene?	**d** future (for what you will do in the future)
E ¿Qué hiciste en tus prácticas laborales?	**e** *quiero / espero* + infinitive (for talking about future plans)

You can express future plans using *ir a* followed by an infinitive:
***Voy a hacer** mis prácticas laborales en el hospital.* (I'm going to do my work experience at the hospital.)
You can also express future plans by using the infinitive after *quiero, espero* and *me gustaría*:
***Quiero/Espero/Me gustaría trabajar** como voluntario.*   I want/hope/would like to work as a volunteer.

(2) Now read sentences **a–e** below which provide answers to the questions in (1).

a Which answer responds to which question? Write the appropriate question letter in the table.

b Now circle (A) the verb in each answer.

c Note how each answer links to the question.

Letter	Answer	How answer links to question
B	**a** Sí, (voy a trabajar) de cajero en una tienda de mi pueblo.	answers question '¿Vas a trabajar ...?' Uses near *future* tense
	b Estudiaré español, pero no estudiaré francés.	
	c Quiero ser ingeniero o electricista porque soy práctico.	
	d Sí, pongo y quito la mesa y a veces paso la aspiradora.	
	e Trabajé en una agencia de viajes. Atendí a los clientes y contesté el teléfono.	

(3) On paper, write your own answers to the questions in (1).

2 How do I check agreements?

Checking agreements is an important way of improving your accuracy when writing in Spanish. You need to:
- make sure verbs agree with the subjects of a sentence
- make sure possessive adjectives agree with the noun they describe
- use *gustar* and similar verbs correctly.

1 Read Miguel's account of his summer job. For each verb (in italics) there are two options. Circle (A) the correct form of each verb so it agrees with its subject.

> Remember to use the correct 'person' of the verb, so that it agrees with the subject.

El verano pasado, **trabajé / trabajó** en una granja de vacas. Mi amigo, Eduardo, también **trabajé / trabajó** allí. Todos los días, **limpiamos / limpiaron** los establos. **Fui / fue** un trabajo duro y sucio. Un día, las vacas se **escapó / escaparon**, pero el granjero **puse / puso** un mensaje en WhatsApp y un vecino **contestó / contestaron** en seguida. Eddie y yo **fuimos / fueron** a su granja y **encontró / encontramos** las vacas. ¡Menos mal!

2 Read Esmae's paragraph about her family. Fill in the gaps using the correct possessive adjectives.

Make sure possessive adjectives agree with the noun they describe:

(my)	**mi** amigo	**mi** amiga	**mis** amigos	**mis** amigas
(his / her / their)	**su** hermano	**su** hermana	**sus** hermanos	**sus** hermanas
(our)	**nuestro** padre	**nuestra** madre	**nuestros** abuelos	**nuestras** abuelas

.......Mi.......... madre trabaja en una empresa pequeña. Le gusta porque ....

compañeros son simpáticos y .... jefe es agradable. .... padre es

profesor en una escuela primaria. Dice que .... alumnos son muy traviesos. Somos

seis en casa porque tengo dos hermanos y .... abuela también vive con nosotros.

3 Adela has written about likes and dislikes in her family. Match up the sentence halves to make a short paragraph.

When talking about likes, remember to use the third person of the verb *gustar*:

Me gusta trabajar de canguro porque me gustan los niños.   I like babysitting because I like children.

Use *me* (me), *le* (him, her, it) *nos* (us) and *les* (them) with *gustar* to identify the person.

Other verbs that follow the same pattern are: *me interesa, me preocupa, me encanta.*

A Me gusta trabajar en	a encanta limpiar.
B me gusta estar	b le gusta cocinar
C A mi padre	c el jardín porque
D y a mi madre le	d al aire libre.
E Pero no nos gusta	e sacar la basura.

How do I improve my spelling?

Although you won't lose marks for the occasional spelling mistake in your writing, too many errors could make your meaning unclear. Here are some ideas to improve your spelling.

Spelling tips: vocabulary

- Only three consonants in Spanish appear as double letters: *cc* (*el accidente*); *ll* (*me llamo*) and *rr* (*el perro*).
- Notice where accents are needed on new words you learn: *el fotógrafo, práctico, árabe, inglés.*
- Remember to write the *ñ* in the correct place: *la mañana, el año.*
- Beware of words that are spelled similarly in English and Spanish, but not quite the same, such as: the future – *el futuro*, necessary – *necesario.*
- Days of the week, months of the year, nationalities and languages don't start with a capital letter in Spanish.

Make a **mental checklist** to help you remember these tips. There are five bullet points. Write an example of each bullet point to help you, such as *perro, simpático, mañana, futuro, febrero.*

1. Read the vocabulary spelling tips above. Then read these two texts written by students about their work. Their texts contain 12 spelling mistakes.

> Trabajo en un taller los <u>sabados</u> por la manana. Tengo que limpiar el suelo en el taler y lavar los coches. Soy bastante practico y me chiflan los coches. En el future quiero ser mecanico o ingeniero.
> Callum

> El ano pasado, hice practicas laborales en una officina. Fue una experiencia positive y muy util porque aprendí a attender a los clientes.
> Bogdan

a Underline Ⓐ the words that are spelled incorrectly.

b Write 🖉 them correctly below.

<u>sábados</u> ....

....

....

2. Look at the spelling tips for verbs. Then read this text written by another student about work experience. Add 🖉 accents to the verbs where necessary.

> El mes pasado, hice mis prácticas laborales en un polideportivo. Trabaje en la recepción y en la oficina. Tuve que contestar el teléfono. También mande correos electrónicos y escribi cartas. Fue una experiencia positiva y mi jefe en la oficina me ayudo mucho. El año que viene, trabajare en un campamento de verano en España y al final, hablare español bastante bien.

Spelling tips: verbs

- Regular verbs in the preterite have an accent on the final letter for first and third person singular ('I' and 'he, she, it'). For example:

  -**ar** verbs: mandar – mand**é**, mand**ó**

  -**er**/-**ir** verbs: escribir – escrib**í**, escrib**ió**

- The preterite endings for irregular verbs don't have accents. For example:

  hacer – hice, hizo

  tener – tuve, tuvo

- Verbs in the **future** have accents on all 'persons' except first person plural ('we'). For example:

  trabajar**é**, trabajar**ás**, trabajar**á**, trabajar**emos**, trabajar**éis**, trabajar**án**

Sample response

To improve your accuracy, you need to:
- use correct verb forms when writing about the past, present or future
- makes sure verbs agree with their subjects, and that possessive adjectives agree with the nouns they describe
- spell words correctly.

Look again at the exam-style writing task on page 49. Then read the sample answer that follows.

> Trabajo los fines de semana en un polideportivo. Trabajo de socorrista en la piscina y también enseño a los niños a nadar. Me va bien porque soy sociable, activo y paciente. Trabajar con niños es divertido. La semana pasada, por ejemplo, una de mis alumnos nadó 20 metros por primera vez. Se quedó muy contenta y yo también.
> El año pasado, hice prácticas laborales en una empresa. Saqué fotocopias y archivé documentos. ¡Qué aburrido! No me gustó nada. En el futuro quiero ser profesor de educación física.

1 Find in the text verbs in each of the following tenses and write 🖉 them below.

   a present: _trabajo_

   b preterite: ....

   c verbs for future plans: (verb + infinitive): ....

2 Note 🖉 two words from the text that tell you whether the writer is male or female.

....

3 Write 🖉 which words tell you whether the child who swam 20 metres for the first time was a girl or a boy.

....

4 Now read another student's response to the same exam-style question. It contains seven mistakes.

   a Find the errors and write 🖉 them in the table next to the relevant mistake description.

   b Now write 🖉 the correct version to complete the table.

> Trabajo de jardinero los sabados y los Domingos. Ayudo a los vecinos en su jardines. Cuido las plantas y corto el césped*. Hace poco, tuve que cortar un árbol, pero encuentro un nido** con pájaros pequeño dentro. No corté el árbol. Es un trabajo que me encanta porque me gusto la naturaleza y me gusta estar al aire libre. El año que viene, va a hacer un aprendizaje*** con una empresa de jardinería.

*grass/lawn   **nest   ***apprenticeship

Type of mistake	Mistake	Correction
incorrect use of capitals	Domingos	domingos
adjective doesn't agree with noun		
possessive adjective doesn't agree with noun		
spelling mistake		
wrong part of verb _gustar_ used		
wrong person of verb used		
wrong tense used		

Your turn!

You are now going to plan and write your own response to the exam-style task from page 49.

the exam-style task from page 49.

Exam-style question

El trabajo

Tu amiga española te pregunta sobre el trabajo que tienes los fines de semana.

Escribe una respuesta a tu amiga.

① Jot down ✐ your ideas in English. Add which tense(s) you might need for that type of answer.

- what work you do now, when and where: ....
  .... Tense: ....

- something interesting that happened at work: ....
  .... Tense: ....

- whether you like or don't like the work and why: ....
  .... Tense: ....

- future work plans: ....
  .... Tense: ....

② Answer ✐ the question. Then check your work using the checklist.

....

....

....

....

....

....

....

....

....

....

....

....

....

....

Checklist In my answers do I ...	✓
answer all the bullet points?	
use the correct verb forms in the right places to talk about past, present and future?	
write the correct preterite endings for regular verbs, including accents on the final letters?	
write the correct preterite forms of irregular verbs?	
make the verbs agree with the subjects?	
make possessive adjectives agree with the words they describe?	
make sure words are spelled correctly using my mental checklist (page 53)?	
make sure accents and special letters are in place (simpático, mañana)?	

Review your skills

Check up

Review your response to the exam-style question on page 55. Tick ✓ the column to show how well you think you have done each of the following.

	Not quite ✓	Nearly there ✓	Got it! ✓
written correct verb forms	☐	☐	☐
checked agreements	☐	☐	☐
improved my spelling	☐	☐	☐

Need more practice?

On paper, plan and write ✏ your response to the exam-style task below.

Exam-style question

Un campamento de verano

Tu amigo español, Fernando, es animador en un campamento. Te dice que el campamento busca gente de habla inglesa para trabajar este verano.

Manda un mensaje para pedir un puesto.

Debes incluir los siguientes puntos:

- tus cualidades personales
- los idiomas que hablas
- tu experiencia y las prácticas laborales que hiciste
- tus ambiciones para el futuro.

Escribe aproximadamente 80–90 palabras **en español**. (20 marks)

How confident do you feel about each of these **skills**? Colour in ✏ the bars.

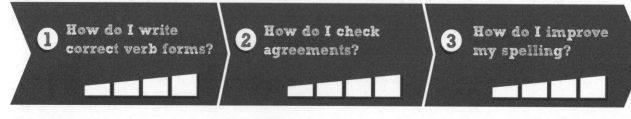

① How do I write correct verb forms?

② How do I check agreements?

③ How do I improve my spelling?

8 Translating into Spanish

This unit will help you to be successful at translating from English into Spanish. The skills you will build are to:

- avoid translating word for word
- use the correct Spanish equivalents for certain verbs and phrases
- make sure your translation is accurate.

In the exam, you will be asked to tackle translating tasks such as the one below. This unit will prepare you to look out for potential problems and translate correctly into Spanish.

In this example a student has translated the English into Spanish correctly.

Exam-style question

El medio ambiente

Traduce las frases **al español**.

(a) Global warming is a very serious problem.

El calentamiento global es un problema muy serio. .... (2)

(b) There is a lot of traffic.

Hay mucho tráfico. .... (2)

(c) I like being a volunteer.

Me gusta ser voluntario. .... (2)

(d) We are going to plant trees near the school and pick up litter.

Vamos a plantar árboles cerca del instituto y a recoger basura del suelo. .... (3)

(e) Last week, I went to school on my bike every day.

La semana pasada, fui al instituto en bici todos los días. .... (3)

(12 marks)

The three key questions in the **skills boosts** will help you translate sentences successfully from English into Spanish.

1 How do I avoid translating word for word?

2 How do I use the correct Spanish equivalents for certain verbs and phrases?

3 How do I make sure my translation is accurate?

Look at the sample student answer on the next page.

Look at a student's translations of the sentences in this exam-style question. The student does not get full marks because there are mistakes in the translations.

Exam-style question

Los problemas del planeta

Traduce las frases siguientes **al español**.

(a) Air pollution is a very serious problem.

-- *Contaminación del aire es un problema* ······ Word missing.

muy serio. ·· **(2)**

(b) There are a lot of homeless people.

Es muchos sin hogar. ·························· **(2)** Wrong verb.

(c) I'm worried about global warming.

Me preocupo el calentamiento global. ······ **(2)** Wrong form of the verb.

(d) You shouldn't throw rubbish on the ground.

No se debe tirar basura en la tierra. ······ **(3)** Avoid translating word for word from English. Learn set phrases.

(e) Last Saturday, I helped to pick up plastic bottles in the park near my house.

El sábado pasado, yo ayudé a recoger botellas de ······ Subject pronouns are not needed before a verb in Spanish. Word missing after *cerca*.

plástico en el parque cerca -- mi casa. ······ **(3)**

(12 marks)

---

① Use the translations in the exam-style question on page 57 to help you correct the sentences in this exam-style question. Write ✐ them below.

- In English we don't use 'the' (definite article) before abstract nouns such as 'poverty', 'unemployment' and 'pollution'. However, in Spanish, we **do** use the definite article: *la pobreza, el desempleo, la contaminación*, etc.
- Remember that you **don't** use the definite article before jobs and professions in Spanish: *Mi tío es granjero y mi tía es enfermera.*

a ··

b ··

c ··

d ··

e ··

How do I avoid translating word for word?

- Certain words and phrases in Spanish cannot be translated literally. You need to know how they are expressed in Spanish.
- Prepositions can be used differently in English and Spanish.

- In Spanish you use the verb 'to have' (*tener*) with age, not the verb 'to be' as in English: *Tengo 15 años.*
- You also use *tener* to express phrases such as 'I'm hot' and 'I'm hungry': *Tengo calor, tengo hambre.*
- Spanish has two verbs for 'to play': *jugar* (to play a sport) and *tocar* (to play a musical instrument).

(1) The English sentences below contain words and phrases that cannot be translated literally.

> Use *desde hace* with the present tense to say how long you have been doing something.

a Circle Ⓐ the correct option to complete the sentences.

b Write 🖉 a note in the space provided to explain your choice.

   i My brother is 24 and he works as a fireman.

     Mi hermano **es** / **tiene** / **hace** 24 años y trabaja de bombero.

     Explanation: *Use 'tener' with age, not 'ser'.*

   ii Today it is sunny and hot.

     Hoy hace sol y **es** / **tiene** / **hace** mucho calor.

     Explanation: ....

   iii Our cat is very thin and he's always hungry.

     Nuestro gato es muy delgado y siempre **tiene** / **es** / **está** hambre.

     Explanation: ....

   iv José plays the guitar quite well but he plays football very badly.

     José **juega** / **toca** / **hace** la guitarra bastante bien, pero juega muy mal al fútbol.

     Explanation: ....

   v Sandra has been learning English for five years.

     Sandra estudia inglés **durante** / **hace** / **desde hace** cinco años.

     Explanation: ....

(2) Complete 🖉 the sentences below by choosing the correct preposition from the box.

a	en	de	por	en	de

> Be careful to use the correct preposition when you translate sentences into Spanish.

a El año pasado, fuimos .... vacaciones a Francia.

b Pablo es el chico más alto .... mi clase.

c .... casa tenemos un perro y dos conejos.

d Reparto periódicos .... la mañana.

e Me gusta ir al insti .... pie, pero es más rápido ir .... bici.

② How do I use the correct Spanish equivalents for certain verbs and phrases?

To avoid making mistakes in translation it's important to notice how certain verbs are used differently in Spanish from the way they are used in English.

① Read the notes in the yellow box below. Then read the sentences that follow and cross out 🖉 the incorrect verb in each case.

Remember that in Spanish:
- you use **tener** ('to have') where in English we use 'to be':
tener éxito	to be successful
tener suerte	to be lucky
tener sueño (calor / frío / hambre / sed, etc.)	to be sleepy (hot / cold / hungry / thirsty, etc.)
- verbs for **eating meals** don't use 'have':
desayunar	to have breakfast
merendar	to have tea
cenar	to have dinner/supper
- you use **reflexive verbs** to talk about **daily routine**:
despertarse	to wake up
levantarse	to get up
ducharse	to have a shower
- **other useful verbs** include:
sacar buenas notas	to get good marks
sacar fotos	to take photos
cuidar a	to look after
salir	to go out

a Los domingos, siempre **salgo / voy fuera** con mis amigos en bicicleta.

b No tengo un trabajo, pero **miro / cuido** al gato y al perro de nuestros vecinos cuando ellos se van de vacaciones.

c Las tiendas de moda Zara y Mango **son / tienen** éxito en todo el mundo.

d De lunes a viernes, **me levanto / me pongo** a las siete menos cuarto.

e Siempre **desayuno / como** un vaso de leche y pan tostado antes de ir al insti.

f **Tienes / Estás** sueño porque te acostaste muy tarde anoche.

g Mi amigo **tiene / es** mucha suerte porque va de vacaciones a Cuba en enero.

h Normalmente, en España **cenamos / comemos cena** entre las nueve y las diez.

i Estoy contenta porque **tuvé / saqué** buenas notas en idiomas y en matemáticas.

② Now translate 🖉 these sentences into Spanish.

a I'm hot and thirsty. ....

b They're very lucky because they've got a big garden. ....

....

c Last night, I went out with my family. ....

d We always have breakfast before we go to school. ....

....

e Tim has to get up early because he's a farmer. ....

....

f I usually get good marks in English. ....

3 **How do I make sure my translation is accurate?**

When translating, be careful with details such as:
- agreement of adjectives
- word order
- using the infinitive after certain verbs.

- Check that adjectives agree with the word they describe and remember they usually come after it:
  Vivimos en un piso pequeño.
- Remember that possessive adjectives *mi, tu, su, nuestro,* etc. are like other adjectives and must agree:
  mi casa, mis amigos, su hermano, sus padres, nuestra vecina, nuestros vecinos
- Words like *mucho* (many, a lot of), *poco* (few, little) and *demasiado* (too, too much / many) must also agree when they describe a noun:
  Hay mucho ruido y mucha contaminación en las ciudades.
  Hay demasiada basura y demasiadas bolsas y botellas de plástico.

Look at pages 3, 11 and 19 for more practice in using adjectives in Spanish.

1 Complete ✏️ these Spanish sentences by translating the English phrases in brackets.

a Vivimos en (a small town) ....

b Nuestros vecinos tienen (lots of dogs) ....

c Su jardín es (too small) ....

d Hay un parque grande cerca de nuestra casa con (lots of plants and flowers)

....

e Tenemos suerte porque hay muy (little traffic and very little pollution)

....

f (Our house) .... tiene placas solares* y ahorramos energía.

g (In our garden) ...., cultivamos ensalada, verduras y fruta.

h (My parents) .... siempre van al trabajo en bicicleta.

*solar panels

2 Read the Spanish sentences below.

In English we often use verbs with **–ing** to talk about likes and future plans. However, to do this in Spanish, you use the infinitive after the conjugated verb:
*Me gusta **participar** en eventos deportivos.*   I like taking part in sports events.

a Find and underline Ⓐ the infinitive verbs in each sentence.

b Match ✏️ each sentence to the correct English translation.

A No me gusta ver basura en la calle.	a I would like to take a gap year.
B Me gustaría tomarme un año sabático.	b I prefer working in a team.
C Prefiero trabajar en equipo.	c I don't like seeing rubbish in the street.
D El año que viene, vamos a hacer un proyecto ecológico en el instituto.	d In the future, I want to study Geography and Environmental Studies.
E En el futuro, quiero estudiar geografía y ciencias ambientales.	e Next year, we're going to do an ecology project at school.

Sample response

To translate effectively, you need to:
- avoid translating word for word
- use the correct Spanish equivalents for certain verbs and phrases
- make sure your translation is accurate.

Do the translated sentences in the sample student answer below follow the three points above about translating effectively?

Exam-style question

Mi ciudad

Traduce las frases siguientes **al español**.

(a) I live in a big city.	(2)
(b) We get on well with our neighbours.	(2)
(c) I like living in the city because my house is near a park.	(2)
(d) Last month, I recycled glass, paper and lots of plastic bottles.	(3)
(e) Next year, my friends and I are going to organise an event about health.	(3)

(12 marks)

(a) *Vivo en una grande ciudad.*

(b) *Nos llevamos bien con nuestro vecinos.*

(c) *Me gusta vivo en la ciudad porque mi casa esta cerca -- un parque.*

(d) *El último mes, reciclo vidrio, papel y muchos botellas de plástico.*

(e) *El año que viene, mi amigos y yo voy a organizo un evento sobre -- salud.*

(1) The translated sentences above contain mistakes, highlighted in yellow. Rewrite ✐ the sentences correctly, using the checklist to help you.

a ....

b ....

c ....

d ....

e ....

Checklist In my answer do I ...	✓
avoid translating literally?	
use the correct Spanish equivalents for set phrases?	
use the correct prepositions?	
position adjectives correctly?	
make adjectives agree with nouns?	
make adjectives such as *mucho, poco* and *demasiado* agree with nouns?	
make possessive adjectives agree with nouns?	
use infinitives after verbs expressing likes and future plans?	
use the correct verb tenses?	
use correct spelling and accents?	

Your turn!

You are now going to write your own response to this exam-style task.

Get back on track

Exam-style question

Mi país y el medio ambiente

Traduce las frases siguientes **al español**.

(a) It's very hot in my country. (2)

(b) There's a lot of traffic. (2)

(c) I'm worried about air pollution. (2)

(d) Last summer, I worked as a volunteer and we picked up a lot of rubbish. (3)

(e) In the future, I want to look after the environment. (3)

(12 marks)

> Correct verb? Possessive adjective?

> Correct verb? Adjective agreement?

> Avoid word-for-word translation. Is a definite article needed?

> Which verb tense? Which persons of the verbs?

> Use infinitive after a verb talking about future plans?

① Answer ✐ the question. Use the hints to help you. Then check your work using the checklist.

a ....

b ....

c ....

d ....

....

e ....

....

Checklist In my answer do I ...	✓
avoid translating literally?	
use the correct Spanish equivalents for set phrases?	
use the correct prepositions?	
position adjectives correctly?	
make adjectives agree with nouns?	
make adjectives such as *mucho*, *poco* and *demasiado* agree with nouns?	
make possessive adjectives agree with nouns?	
use infinitives after verbs expressing likes and future plans?	
use the correct verb tenses?	
use correct spelling and accents?	

Review your skills

Check up

Review your response to the exam-style question on page 63. Tick ✓ the column to show how well you think you have done each of the following.

	Not quite ✓	Nearly there ✓	Got it! ✓
avoided translating word for word	☐	☐	☐
used the correct Spanish equivalents for verbs and phrases	☐	☐	☐
made sure my translation is accurate	☐	☐	☐

Need more practice?

On paper, plan and write ✎ your responses to the exam-style tasks below.

Exam-style question

Mi pueblo

Traduce las frases siguientes **al español**.

(a) I live in a small town near the beach. (2)

(b) It's very hot in July and August. (2)

(c) There isn't much traffic, so I usually cycle to school. (2)

(d) Last week, we went to Barcelona with our teachers. (3)

(e) Next year, we're going to organise a football tournament to raise money. (3)

(12 marks)

Exam-style question

La salud

Traduce las frases siguientes **al español**.

(a) I think health is very important. (2)

(b) I never smoke because it's not good for your health. (2)

(c) We eat well at home and I do sports every day. (2)

(d) Last weekend, I took part in a charity sports event. (3)

(e) Next year, I want to take part in a half-marathon. (3)

(12 marks)

How confident do you feel about each of these **skills**? Colour in ✎ the bars.

1 How do I avoid translating word for word?

2 How do I use the correct Spanish equivalents for certain verbs and phrases?

3 How do I make sure my translation is accurate?

⑨ Using impressive language

This unit will help you to use impressive language in your written answers. The skills you will build are to:

- use interesting vocabulary
- use grammar to best effect
- create opportunities to use more complex language.

In the exam, you will be asked to tackle a writing task such as the one below. This unit will prepare you to plan and write your own response to this question, using language that's not just accurate but also impressive.

Exam-style question

El futuro del planeta

Escriba usted un artículo para la revista del instituto para convencer* a los lectores de nuestra responsabilidad para con el planeta.

Debe incluir los puntos siguientes:

- cuáles son los mayores problemas medioambientales en su barrio
- qué piensa que se debe hacer para resolver los problemas y por qué
- lo que hizo usted recientemente para llevar una vida más verde
- sus planes para ser solidario.

Justifique sus ideas y sus opiniones.

Escriba aproximadamente 130–150 palabras **en español**.   (28 marks)

*convencer (a alguien de) – to convince (someone of something)

The three key questions in the **skills boosts** will help you use impressive language.

1 How do I make sure I use interesting vocabulary?

2 How do I use grammar to best effect?

3 How do I create opportunities to use more complex language?

Look at the sample student answer on the next page.

Read Teresa's answer to the question on page 65 and answer the questions below.

Para mí el problema medioambiental más serio en mi barrio es la contaminación del aire, ya que afecta la salud. Creo que el transporte público no es bueno y por eso hay demasiado tráfico y tanta contaminación. También me preocupa la basura.

Pienso que lo más importante es reducir la contaminación. Se debería mejorar la red de transporte público en la ciudad. También hay que ir en bici y no usar el coche cuando no es necesario. Es esencial hacer campañas publicitarias sobre la importancia de reciclar porque la basura contamina los mares y los ríos.

En mi opinión, todos podemos cuidar el medio ambiente. Por ejemplo, la semana pasada decidí participar en un proyecto para limpiar el barrio. Mis compañeros y yo recogimos papeles y botellas por todo el parque.

Me preocupa muchísimo el futuro del planeta, así que voy a estudiar ecología en la universidad. También me gustaría trabajar como voluntario en un proyecto para plantar más árboles porque la destrucción de los bosques es un problema muy grave.

(1) Tick ✓ the four statements that are correct. Then rewrite 🖉 on paper the four that are wrong.

a Teresa thinks air pollution is a health hazard.

b She is also worried about the lack of recycling facilities.

c Teresa believes improved transport links will reduce pollution.

d She thinks there should be advertising campaigns about the importance of recycling.

e Teresa thinks we should all use less energy.

f Teresa helped clean up her local river.

g She plans to go to university.

h She would like to volunteer in a water aid project.

(2) To succeed in extended writing tasks you need to plan carefully. Find key points that Teresa makes for each bullet point and note 🖉 the phrases she uses in the table.

Bullet points	Key points
• los mayores problemas medioambientales en su barrio	la contaminación del aire
• qué se debe hacer para resolver los problemas	
• lo que hizo para llevar una vida más verde	
• sus planes para ser solidario	

How do I make sure I use interesting vocabulary?

Practise using varied and precise vocabulary. Do this by:
- learning words as part of a topic
- collecting synonyms
- learning phrases rather than isolated words.

You will remember words better if you group them by topic. Of course, many words can be used across different topics.

1 The box below contains words from Teresa's text on page 66. Circle Ⓐ the ones that relate to the environment topic.

> medioambiental   la contaminación   la salud   el transporte público   el tráfico
>
> la basura   el coche   los mares   los ríos   cuidar   limpiar
>
> los papeles   ecología   voluntario   destrucción

2 When you note down vocabulary, try to expand your range by noting synonyms as well – words that mean the same. Read the text on page 66 again and note ✐ synonyms for the following words and phrases.

a la polución — *la contaminación*

b los residuos — ....

c ensuciar — ....

d informar al público — ....

e proteger — ....

f la naturaleza — ....

g actuar junto — ....

h la tierra — ....

i la pérdida — ....

3 Learn vocabulary as part of a phrase rather than as isolated words whenever possible.

Link ✐ verbs **A–H** to nouns **a–h** to produce key phrases for this topic. One has been done for you.

> Verbs play an important part in your stock of vocabulary. Learn the important infinitives to have a strong knowledge base.

A ahorrar	a la contaminación
B separar	b bolsas de plástico
C comprar	c productos ecológicos
D proteger	d el calentamiento global
E reducir	e la basura
F luchar contra	f agua
G apagar	g la luz
H no usar	h el medio ambiente

2 **How do I use grammar to best effect?**

You have done a lot of practice to get your grammar right. Now use your knowledge to impress. Try to:
- mix time frames (present, preterite and imperfect, future)
- vary the verb forms so you don't just use *yo*.

Read this very plain paragraph about someone's lifestyle.

> *Me gustaría llevar una vida sana. Suelo comer comida rápida, me gusta. Fumo cigarrillos. Es un asco.*

> To use a wider range of tenses, you could say:
> - what happened in the past – using the preterite for a completed event, and the imperfect for descriptions and repeated actions
> - what will happen in the future – using *ir* + infinitive.

① Think of ways you could improve the paragraph. For example:

a Mention ✏️ what you had to eat yesterday, using the **preterite** tense.

....

b Add ✏️ a comment about what you ate, using the **imperfect** tense (e.g. *había, comía, me gustaba*).

....

c Mention ✏️ how you are going to change your lifestyle, using the **near future** tense.

....

② On paper, rewrite ✏️ the following paragraph to make it more interesting, adding references to past and future.

> *Me gustaría llevar una vida sana. Bebo demasiado alcohol, me emborracho cuando salgo de fiesta. No hago ejercicio. Prefiero dormir.*

Now look at texts A and B. Notice how text B uses varied verb forms, not just *yo* forms.

A
> *Soy muy ecológico. En casa reciclo todo lo posible. Siempre uso productos ecológicos para limpiar. No uso el coche, voy en bici o uso el transporte público.*

→

B
> *Mi familia y yo somos muy ecológicos. En casa reciclamos todo lo posible. Mis padres siempre usan productos ecológicos. Mi madre no usa el coche, va en bici al trabajo.*

③ On paper, adapt ✏️ the following paragraph by varying the verb forms, as in text B above.

> *Quiero proteger el medio ambiente. No malgasto el agua. Hago todo lo posible para ahorrar energía. Desenchufo los aparatos eléctricos y apago la luz cuando salgo de una habitación.*

Take care with verb endings when you write.

	Present tense verb endings					
	Common irregular verbs			Regular -ar verbs	Regular -er verbs	Regular -ir verbs
	ser	ir	hacer	reciclar	deber	decidir
yo	soy	voy	hago	reciclo	debo	decido
el/ella/usted	es	va	hace	recicla	debe	decide
nosotros	somos	vamos	hacemos	reciclamos	debemos	decidimos
ellos/ellas	son	van	hacen	reciclan	deben	deciden

3 How do I create opportunities to use more complex language?

Take opportunities to add information and detail to your writing. Give opinions and justify them to add emphasis to your points. Remember the FEOR technique: give **F**acts, **E**xamples, **O**pinions and **R**easons.

1 Make your writing sound more convincing by using phrases such as those in the table:

Para mí… En mi opinión… Creo que… Pienso que…	… el mayor problema (global / del medio ambiente / social) … lo más preocupante … el problema más serio … el peor problema … la mejor solución	es + noun (e.g. la contaminación)
	… hay que … (no) se debería	+ infinitive (e.g. reciclar)

Read sentences **a–d**, then rewrite ✍ them using the phrases above. There are several possibilities.

Ejemplo: *Para mí, lo más preocupante es el calentamiento global.*

a El calentamiento global es un problema serio.

....

b Me preocupa la contaminación.

....

c Es necesario reducir la basura y reciclar más.

....

d Tenemos que hacer proyectos medioambientales.

....

2 When writing, remember to give Facts, Examples, Opinions and Reasons (FEOR).

a Read the text below. Decide whether the phrases are F, E, O or R and note ✍ the appropriate letter in the answer box. (Some phrases can be both Fact and Example.)

Creo que el problema más serio del planeta es la destrucción del medio ambiente. ☐ *En las ciudades, hay contaminación del aire* ☐ *y en los ríos y en el mar hay demasiada basura.* ☐
Además, hay miles de animales y plantas en peligro de extinción. ☐ *Pienso que todos tenemos que trabajar para proteger la naturaleza* ☐ *porque si no lo hacemos ahora, no vamos a salvar el planeta.* ☐ *Se debería hacer campañas publicitarias para animar* a todos a ser más responsables* ☐ *porque si todos los hacemos, cambiaremos el mundo.* ☐

*to encourage

b Read the text again. Find and note ✍ down:

i two phrases used to give an opinion: ....

....

ii a word that introduces a reason: ....

iii a word that introduces an additional example or reason: ....

Sample response

To impress with your written answers, you need to:
- use interesting vocabulary
- use grammar to best effect
- create opportunities to use more complex language.

Now look at this exam-style writing task, similar to the one on page 65. Then read one student's answer.

similar to the one on page 65

Exam-style question

Los problemas en nuestra ciudad o región

Escriba usted un artículo para la revista del instituto sobre los problemas sociales locales.

Debe incluir los puntos siguientes:
- cuáles son los mayores problemas sociales en su ciudad o región
- qué piensa que se debe hacer para solucionar los problemas
- algo que hizo recientemente como voluntario
- los planes para eventos solidarios en el futuro.

Justifique sus ideas y sus opiniones.

Escriba aproximadamente 130–150 palabras **en español**.   (28 marks)

Para mí el problema más preocupante es la desigualdad social. Vivimos en una ciudad con muchas atracciones turísticas y con una economía fuerte, sin embargo, hay desempleo, sobre todo entre los jóvenes y hay mucha gente sin hogar. Pienso que se debería crear más oportunidades de trabajo y construir más pisos y casas de precio moderado.

Otros problemas serios en nuestra ciudad son la drogadicción y el alcohol. Creo que se debería organizar campañas y proyectos para informar a la gente de los peligros de tomar drogas y beber alcohol. Además pienso que vale la pena hacer más actividades deportivas y sociales para unir a la gente.

El año pasado, trabajé como animador en un curso de verano para niños del barrio. Hicimos actividades deportivas y también había clases de cocina. Este verano, vamos a participar en un curso de música y baile para jóvenes que terminará con un concierto solidario.

Pienso que en el futuro, se debería organizar más eventos solidarios para recaudar dinero para ayudar a las familias en paro.

1. a. In the text, circle (A) three different phrases that introduce the writer's opinion.
   b. Highlight:
      i. two phrases in the preterite to say what the writer did last summer using verb forms 'I' and 'we'
      ii. a phrase starting with a verb in the imperfect
      iii. two phrases about future plans using verb forms other than *yo*.

2. The table below lists three problems mentioned in the text. Find and note down:
   a. the Spanish terms for the three problems
   b. the writer's suggested solutions to these problems, each starting with a verb in the infinitive.

Problem (English)	Problem (Spanish)	Solution
unemployment		
homeless people		
drug addiction and alcohol		

Your turn!

You are now going to plan and write your response to the exam-style task on page 65.

Look at the question again.

Exam-style question

El futuro del planeta

Escriba usted un artículo para la revista del instituto para convencer a los lectores de nuestra responsabilidad para con el planeta.

Debe incluir los puntos siguientes:

- cuáles son los mayores problemas medioambientales en su barrio
- qué piensa que se debe hacer para resolver los problemas y por qué
- lo que hizo usted recientemente para llevar una vida más verde
- sus planes para ser solidario.

Justifique sus ideas y sus opiniones.

Escriba aproximadamente 130–150 palabras **en español**.   (28 marks)

(1) First jot down 🖊 your ideas.

a   the most serious environmental problems in your area:

....

b   what you think should be done to solve the problems:

....

c   what you did recently to be environmentally friendly:

....

d   your plans for getting involved in charity events in the future:

....

(2) Answer 🖊 the question. Then check your work using the checklist.

Checklist	
In my answer do I ...	✓
use a wide range of vocabulary?	
use synonyms to avoid repetition?	
use topic-specific verb phrases?	
develop ideas using a range of tenses?	
mix the time frames and use a range of verb forms (not just *yo*)?	
add emphasis to my ideas and opinions?	
give facts, examples, opinions and reasons?	

Review your skills

Check up

Review your response to the exam-style question on page 71. Tick ⊘ the column to show how well you think you have done each of the following.

	Not quite ⊘	Nearly there ⊘	Got it! ⊘
used interesting vocabulary	☐	☐	☐
used grammar to best effect	☐	☐	☐
created opportunities to use more complex language	☐	☐	☐

Need more practice?

On paper, plan and write ⊘ your response to the task below.

Exam-style question

Un festival musical y medioambiental

Usted quiere trabajar como voluntario en un festival solidario que recaudará dinero para proyectos medioambientales.

Escriba a los organizadores para convencerles de su interés en el trabajo.

Debe incluir los puntos siguientes:

• lo que más le preocupa del medioambiente

• por qué quiere participar en el festival

• su experiencia como voluntario en proyectos verdes y eventos solidarios

• sus ideas para promover la participación de los jóvenes en la protección del planeta en el futuro.

Justifique sus ideas y sus opiniones.

Escriba aproximadamente 130–150 palabras **en español**. (28 marks)

How confident do you feel about each of these **skills**? Colour in ⊘ the bars.

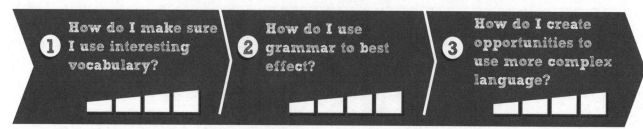

1 How do I make sure I use interesting vocabulary?

2 How do I use grammar to best effect?

3 How do I create opportunities to use more complex language?

Answers

Unit 1

Page 2

(1) Incorrect statements: **a, d**

(2) A c B a C f D e E b/d F d/b

(3) 1 who is in the photo

2 where they are

3 what the weather is like

4 opinion

5 opinion

6 reason

Page 3

(1) (a)

personas	lugares	vacaciones
joven	histórico	inolvidable
activo	turístico	activo
mayor	cómodo	relajante
simpático	malo	malo
preocupado	bonito	barato
contento	barato	bueno
triste	lujoso	desastroso
bonito	bueno	
	desastroso	
	moderno	
	ruidoso	
	inolvidable	

(2) En esta foto hay unos jóvenes **contentos**. Están en una playa **bonita**. Hace **buen** tiempo. Son unas vacaciones **inolvidables**.

Page 4

(1) Circled: en el centro, turística, mucho, y, muy, siempre

(2) (a) en el centro

(b) mucho

(c) A la izquierda

(d) también

(e) muy

(f) debajo

(g) porque

(h) por eso

Page 5

(1) (a)/(b) Suggested answers

	phrase/word in text	note
masculine singular:	verano	'-o' is a common ending for masculine nouns.
masculine plural:	unos jóvenes	'unos' is the masculine plural for 'some'.
feminine singular:	una ciudad	'una' is the feminine singular word for 'a'.
feminine plural:	vacaciones	'-es' is the plural ending of 'vacación', which is a feminine word.

(2) (a) es, (b) son, (c) lleva, (d) están, (e) come, (f) compra, (g) habla, (h) visita

(3) A Circled: Las chicas (están) en un parque. Hace (muchas) sol. (Practicamos) yoga. Creo que es (divertidas).

B Correct versions: están, mucho, Practican, divertido

Page 6

(1) (a) prepositions of place: (X)

(b) adjectives: (✓)

(c) adverbs: (X)

(d) connectives: (X)

(2) It is not a very convincing answer to the task.

Suggested justification:

There could be a preposition of place to say where the people are in the picture, and a location could be suggested. There could be an adjective to describe the people. There could be an adverb to describe the weather. Connectives could be used to link the sentences. Reasons could be given for the opinions.

(3) Suggested answer:

Hay dos chicos y dos chicas en el centro de la foto. Están en una ciudad turística. Hace mucho sol y creo que es verano. En mi opinión, las vacaciones en una ciudad son aburridas porque prefiero la playa.

Page 7

(2) En la foto hay una familia. Hace frío y llevan chaqueta, guantes y gorro. Es invierno y hay mucha nieve. Están de vacaciones de esquí en la montaña. Me encanta esquiar porque es divertido y además, haces ejercicio.

Page 8

Hay dos chicos en la foto. Están jugando al voleibol en la playa. Es verano y hace sol, por eso llevan bañador. En mi opinión, hacer deporte al aire libre y cerca del mar es muy saludable.

Unit 2

Page 10

(1) (a) school

(b) favourite subjects

(c) The best thing

(d) what you are going to do next week

(e) teachers

(f) opinion / uniform

(g) extracurricular activities / last week

(h) what are you going to do / his visit to the school

(2) Sample answer A

(a) The school is a mixed private school.

(b) It is quite far from London. (X)

c The student likes Biology and English. ⊗

d The sport centre is quite small. ⊗

e The student will go on a trip next week. ⊗

Sample answer B

f The student doesn't get on with his teachers because they are strict. ⊗

g They have to wear uniform at school.

h The student thinks wearing a uniform is boring. ⊗

i Last week he went swimming.

j They will go to see a play in the afternoon.

Page 11

1
a delicious / disgusting

b strong / weak

c clever / stupid

d open-minded / closed-minded

e marvellous / terrible

f complicated / simple

g lazy / hardworking

h fair / unfair

i clean / dirty

j quiet / noisy

Page 12

1 <u>Lo mejor</u> de mi instituto es que es moderno y las instalaciones son nuevas. Pero (lo peor) es que es demasiado grande. <u>Me mola el polideportivo porque</u> está bien equipado, pero (por desgracia) no hay piscina. <u>Me encantan</u> los profesores, pero ponen muchos deberes. ¡Qué horror! (Detesto) el uniforme porque es muy formal. (Odio) la corbata en particular. <u>Me chifla</u> la variedad de actividades extraescolares y toco el violín en la orquesta. ¡Es superdivertido! <u>Me gustó</u> mucho participar en un concurso nacional el trimestre pasado. No ganamos pero, ¡fue flipante!

2 **Me chiflan** las actividades en mi instituto porque son **variadas** y te ayudan a **aprender cosas nuevas.** Los jueves voy al club de natación. Voy desde hace un año. **Me encanta** porque el trimestre pasado **gané un trofeo. ¡Fue genial!** También toco el violín en la orquesta. **Es creativo** pero no voy a continuar el año que viene porque **no tengo tiempo.**

Page 13

1 Durante las vacaciones fui a Londres con mi clase de español y participamos en un intercambio. Creo que los intercambios son (muy) buenos porque te ayudan a aprender (más) inglés. Me alojé en la casa de mi compañera inglesa, Sofie. (Desafortunadamente) la visita fue (bastante) difícil porque no hablo (bien) el inglés y la familia era (un poco) antipática. También visitamos el centro pero en mi opinión Londres es (demasiado) caro para estudiantes como nosotros.

2 Suggested answers (shown in bold below)

Durante el intercambio visitamos el instituto de nuestros compañeros. Los estudiantes ingleses tienen que llevar uniforme. ¡Qué horror! Creo que el uniforme es **muy** feo y **demasiado** formal. Las clases eran un **poco** largas y

los profesores eran **bastante** estrictos. Comimos en el comedor y pienso que la comida inglesa es **más** variada que la comida española. Me gustó **mucho** la experiencia.

3
a No me gusta llevar uniforme porque es incómodo. La corbata, por ejemplo, no es práctica.

b La comida en el comedor es buena porque es variada. Los postres, por ejemplo, son deliciosos.

c Me mola ir a los clubs extraescolares porque aprendes cosas nuevas. Por ejemplo, el año pasado aprendí a tocar la guitarra.

d Es flipante participar en concursos porque te ayuda a mejorar tu técnica. Por ejemplo, el trimestre pasado gané un trofeo.

Page 14

1 The text doesn't show convincing opinions. Possible justifications for this are:

The student doesn't use varied phrases to introduce opinions, for example, repeating me gusta and no me gusta.

The adjectives the student uses are repetitive and imprecise.

The student doesn't use a variety of qualifiers and adverbs to reinforce their opinions.

The student doesn't give reasons for their opinions, for example by using porque.

The student doesn't give examples to back up the reasons for their opinions.

The student doesn't give any opinions about past events, only about the present.

2 Suggested answers:

Pienso que llevo un uniforme bastante cómodo ya que es muy fácil ponérmelo. Llevo una camisa blanca, corbata a rayas, pantalón gris y zapatos negros. Además de un jersey azul.

Las actividades extraescolares son variadas debido a que hay mucho para hacer. Me gusta jugar al baloncesto, al hockey y al tenis. Puedo practicar natación también porque hay una piscina grande y muy guay.

Durante tu visita, creo que vamos a ir a una excursión con la clase. En mi opinión va a ser muy guay porque visitaremos sitios de interés. Por ejemplo, la catedral, un museo de videojuegos y muchos lugares más.

Page 15

1
a Bullet point 1: present; Bullet point 2: present; Bullet point 3: present; Bullet point 4: near future/future

b Possible answers

Mi instituto:

school description: En mi instituto hay…/Mi instituto tiene…/Mi instituto es…, aulas, un gimnasio, una biblioteca, un comedor, un campo de fútbol

subjects: el inglés, la informática, los idiomas, las matemáticas

best thing about school: lo mejor es…, lo bueno es que…

sports day: jugar a…, participar en…, nadar, un partido de fútbol, un torneo, ganar un trofeo

opinion words (formal): me encanta(n), me interesa(n), odio, prefiero

adjectives: grande, pequeño/a, amplio/a, moderno/a, antiguo/a, favorito/a, fácil

El instituto:

teachers description: Mi profe (de inglés) es…, severo/a, aburrido/a, gracioso/a, simpático/a

uniform: Llevo…, una camisa, una corbata, unos pantalones, una falda, una chaqueta

extracurricular activities: fui al club de (fotografía/teatro), participé en un concierto, cantamos en el coro

activities during visit: vamos a ver una película, vamos a participar en un torneo de tenis, vas a asistir a mi clase de inglés

opinion words (informal): me chifla(n), me mola(n), guay, flipante, fatal

adjectives: gris, azul, blanco/a, a rayas, bonito/a, feo/a, práctico/a, (in)cómodo/a

c Opinions required about:

Mi instituto: favourite subjects, best thing about school

El instituto: what teachers are like, school uniform

Page 16

Suggested answers

Un intercambio en el instituto

Estudio español desde hace tres años. Además, estudio ciencias, matemáticas y otras asignaturas.

Mi instituto tiene laboratorios y una biblioteca. Hay un polideportivo y también un comedor.

Tenemos que llevar uniforme y no podemos usar los móviles en clase. Por lo general, las normas son razonables, aunque creo que llevar uniforme es demasiado formal.

Durante el intercambio me alojaré y comeré en casa de unos amigos españoles.

Un viaje escolar

Mi instituto es moderno y tiene novecientos estudiantes. Hay buenas instalaciones y también ofrece muchos clubs extraescolares.

En abril hice un viaje escolar a Madrid. Nos alojamos con familias españolas. Todas las mañanas teníamos clases de español en un centro de idiomas. Por las tardes íbamos de excursión

Lo bueno del viaje es que aprendí mucho español. También me gustó ir de compras porque la ropa es más barata que en el Reino Unido. Lo malo es que no me gustaba la comida.

En el próximo viaje habrá más variedad de comida y más excursiones. Me parece muy buena idea, porque así todos los estudiantes podrán elegir. Además, haremos más deporte al aire libre. ¡Eso es muy sano!

Unit 3

Page 18

① Las redes sociales

- uses WhatsApp, very practical
- uses mobile every day, sends messages to friends and parents
- addictive, expensive
- to download music, watch videos

② La vida de hoy (any 2 of the following)

- Felipe, classmate, they play football every day
- watched American film, on TV, liked it, actors good
- loves music, downloads/shares new songs with friends
- plans to skype friends, share photos of a recent trip

Page 19

① Mis aplicaciones preferidas **son** Instagram y WhatsApp. También **uso** Facebook de vez en cuando. A mi amiga, Gemma, le encanta Facebook y **publica** mensajes y fotos nuevas todos los días. Lo malo de la tecnología móvil **es** que cuando el móvil no **funciona**, ¡es un desastre!

② a un chico divertido

b una película americana

c los actores buenos

d las canciones nuevas

③ WhatsApp es **la** aplicación más económica y más práctica para mandar mensajes a **los** amigos. Y como siempre tienes **el** móvil contigo, siempre estás en contacto. Pero para escribir emails, ver vídeos y subir **las** fotos de tus vacaciones, es más cómodo usar **el** ordenador.

Page 20

① **a**/**b**/**c** Right-hand column contains possible answers.

idea	example	translation	comments
play a sport	Jugamos al fútbol.	We play football.	Spanish has a + el (al) or a la before a sport with jugar.
age	Tengo 15 años.	I'm 15.	In Spanish the verb 'to have' (tener) is used with age, not the verb 'to be'.
how long ago	Fuimos a Barcelona hace dos semanas.	We went to Barcelona two weeks ago.	Spanish uses hace plus a time expression, dos semanas. English uses a time expression, 'two weeks', before 'ago'.
expressing likes	Me gusta compartir fotos en Instagram.	I like sharing photos on Instagram.	Spanish uses the third person form of the verb gustar, so me gusta means 'it is pleasing to me'.
word order	Mi red social preferida es Facebook.	My favourite social network is Facebook.	An adjective usually comes after the noun it describes.
watching TV, film	Veo vídeos en YouTube.	I watch videos on YouTube.	In Spanish the verb ver, 'to see', is used with TV, films and videos, meaning 'to watch'.
weather	Hace buen tiempo.	The weather is good.	In Spanish, the verb hacer is used to describe weather.

Page 21

1 **a**/ b/ c

formal	informal
Estimado señor	Hola
guay	magnífico
Atentamente	Hasta luego
Usted	tú
sus profesores	tus profes
la televisión	la tele
el instituto	el insti

2
  a Me llevo **superbién** con mi amiga, Julia.

  b Estoy haciendo un ejercicio de matemáticas. ¡Qué rollo!

  c Iremos de viaje a Sevilla en junio. ¡Qué guay!

  d Me gusta mucho leer y **me molan** las novelas de vampiros.

  e Fuimos a un partido en el Nou Camp y Messi marcó dos goles. ¡Fue **flipante**!

3
  a qué le gusta comer   what you like to eat

  b qué idiomas habla   what languages you speak

  c cuándo va a viajar   when you are going to travel

  d cuál es su película favorita   what your favourite film is

Page 22

1 **a**/ b Corrected text, with type of correction shown in blue boxes:

Estimado señor

Me gusta /Me gusto V leer revistas y las biografías de deportistas porque me interesa el deporte. Leo los fines de semana y durante los / las A vacaciones. Prefiero leo / leer V e-books porque son más transportable / transportables ADJ que el / los A libros en papel. Durante las próximas vacaciones leeré / leo V la biografía del atleta español Kílian Jornet.

Atentamente / Hasta luego R

Maya Warren

2
  a opening greeting: Hola

  b two informal vocabulary items: una peli, en bici

  c informal 'you' form: ¿Y tú, cómo estás?

  d closing message: Hasta luego

Page 24

Suggested answers

Las relaciones con la familia y los amigos

Estimado Señor:

Somos cuatro en mi familia: mi padre, mi madre, mi hermano y yo. Me llevo muy bien con mis padres, pero me peleo con mi hermano a veces. Mi mejor amiga se llama Laura. Es inteligente y simpática. En las próximas vacaciones, vamos a ir a un festival de música.

Atentamente:

Emily

Un informe sobre la tecnología móvil

Hola, Elisabet.

Mis amigos usan Instagram y Facebook para compartir fotos y publicar mensajes. Todos usamos WhatsApp porque es una aplicación muy práctica y porque es gratis mandar y recibir mensajes. La semana pasada, por ejemplo, usé WhatsApp todos los días para contactar con mis amigos. Mis padres usan WhatsApp, pero no usan Facebook. Mi padre usa Spotify para descargar y escuchar música. Mis abuelos me mandan mensajes en el móvil y a veces hablamos por Skype. Esta noche, a lo mejor, voy a ver una película en el ordenador.

Hasta luego:

Sam

Unit 4

Page 26

1
  a She likes sport and she's quite an active person.

  b basketball, hockey, swimming, running and tennis

  c Rafael Nadal, because she admires him for being a good tennis player and because he has won many championships.

  d On Saturday morning, she went out on her bike, then she swam and, after that, she did some gym work. In the afternoon she went shopping with her parents.

  e On Sunday she did nothing.

  f Next year she wants to take part in a mini-triathlon, so she's going to do more running.

2
  a ayer, los martes, el año que viene

  b ha ganado

  c salí (en bici), nadé, hice gimnasia, fui (de compras)

  d voy a correr

Page 27

1 Ticked: **a**, **b**, **c**

2 A c

  B a

  C d

  D b

3 1 el año pasado

  2 el mes pasado

  3 hace dos semanas

  4 la semana pasada

  5 ayer

  6 mañana

  7 el fin de semana que viene

  8 el mes que viene

Page 28

1
  a false: Generalmente, los fines de semana me quedo en casa.

  b true: el sábado pasado, salí al parque por la noche con mi familia.

  c false: fuimos a ver una película al cine al aire libre.

d true: Lo pasé bomba

e true: la película fue genial

f false: mi padre se durmió y no vio el final de la peli.

g true: ¡Por suerte no roncó!

2 Generalmente, los fines de semana (me quedo) en casa. (Veo) la tele, (escucho) música y (descanso). <u>Sin embargo</u>, el sábado pasado, salí al parque por la noche con mi familia. <u>Pero</u> se no fuimos a pasear, fuimos a ver una película al cine al aire libre. Lo pasé bomba porque la película fue genial y además, hacía buen tiempo. <u>Desafortunadamente</u>, mi padre se durmió y no vio el final de la peli. ¡Por suerte no roncó!

Page 29

1 **a** Underlined: lo pasé superbién, salí, fuimos, jugué, ganó, fui, se vistieron de, tocaron, fue

b I had a great time: lo pasé superbién

I went out: salí

we went: fuimos

I played: jugué

(the team) won: ganó

I went: fui

they dressed as: se vistieron de

they played: tocaron

it was: fue

2 Correct verb forms in bold:

Hola, Roberto.

¡Qué fin de semana más guay! Gracias por las fotos de la fiesta. Pues, yo el fin de sábado pasado, **vi** una película en la tele. Luego **fui** al polideportivo y **jugué** al balonmano. Después **salí** al parque a pasear al perro, **toqué** la guitarra un rato y **descansé** bastante. El domingo mi hermana **jugó** un partido de voleibol y luego **fuimos** todos a comer a casa de mis abuelos.

Hasta pronto.

Alberto

Page 30

1

using an opportunity to link a past event with the present	Mis deportes preferidos son el rugby… vi un partido estupendo
using a time phrase to refer to the past	el año pasado, la semana pasada, hace poco
using a past event as contrast	No soy muy deportista pero el año pasado, gané un campeonato de ping-pong en el insti
giving an opinion about an event in the past	Fue genial
using the correct preterite endings for regular verbs	gané, pasé, cocinamos, no nos peleamos
correctly spelling preterite verbs that are irregular / have spelling changes	fue, dormimos
varying the verb forms (that is, not just using first person singular)	dormimos, cocinamos, no nos peleamos

Page 32

Suggested answer

El tiempo libre, tus intereses y tú

En mi tiempo libre, para descansar, suelo escuchar música y leer. También me gusta ver vídeos en YouTube porque son divertidos, pero no veo mucho la televisión. Mis pasatiempos preferidos son jugar al fútbol y tocar la guitarra y el teclado. La semana pasada, fui a un concierto de música electrónica. Fue fantástico. El sábado, jugué en un partido de fútbol y mi equipo ganó. El fin de semana que viene, voy a ir al cine con mis amigos.

Unit 5
Page 34

1 **a** P

b P

c Pret

d F

2 **a** by the sea

b lovely views

c quite cold and windy

d two weeks ago

e it's the best thing about the place

f rest/relax

3 Mi pueblo está situado al lado del mar y está rodeado de montañas. Tiene unas vistas muy bonitas. El clima es variable, hace sol, pero también llueve a menudo. En invierno hace bastante frío y viento. Hace dos semanas visité un castillo que está en el centro del pueblo, creo que es lo mejor de este lugar; además del paisaje. El próximo fin de semana, si hace buen tiempo, mis amigos y yo iremos a la costa y descansaremos en la playa. ¡Será guay!

Present

Preterite

Future

Page 35

1 **b**, **d**, **f**

2 A c, B a, C d, D b

3 **a** el mes que viene

b en el verano

c el fin de semana que viene

d durante las vacaciones

4 A d

B a

C b

D c

Page 36

1 ¡Hola!

Este fin de semana **haré** camping con mi familia en la sierra cerca de mi ciudad. **Disfrutaré** de paisajes impresionantes y mis padres y yo **practicaremos** senderismo. Si hace calor, **naderemos** en los lagos y mi madre **leerá** una novela al sol. Mi padre **preparará** la comida y **comeremos** al aire libre. El domingo **iremos** de excursión y **visitaremos** unas cuevas con estalagmitas. ¡**Será** flipante!

2 **a** El mes que viene yo (fue) a Madrid con mi clase. Nos (alojar) en una pensión por cinco noches. (Visitaron) el museo del Prado y el Parque del Retiro. Lo mejor (son) la visita guiada al Estadio Bernabeu porque me mola el fútbol. El domingo por la mañana mis compañeros y yo (irá) al mercado del Rastro y yo compré (recuerdo)s. Una tarde nosotros salir a una (churr)ería y comer chur(ros) c(on) chocolate. ¡Qué rico! La visita son superdiv(erti)da.

b i iré

ii alojaremos

iii Visitaremos

iv será

v iremos

vi compraré

vii saldremos

viii comeremos

ix será

Page 37

1 **a** Underline: si hace buen tiempo, jugaré al fútbol; si llueve, cogeremos el autobús; si tenemos hambre, comeremos una hamburguesa; si viene mi primo a mi casa, iremos a la bolera; si termino pronto, mi hermano y yo iremos a la pista de hielo

b Translations: if the weather is good, I will play football; if it rains, we'll catch the bus; if we're hungry, we'll eat a burger; if my cousin comes to my house, we'll go to the bowling alley; if I finish early, my brother and I will go to the ice rink

Page 38

1

	A	B
time phrases to indicate the future		El próximo fin de semana Después
something that the writer is planning to do	haremos muchas cosas iremos en autocar a un parque temático	visitaremos un pueblo en la costa haremos deportes acuáticos compraremos patatas fritas las comeremos en la playa
a variety of verbs in the future tense	haremos, iremos, será	visitaremos, haremos, practicaré, compraremos, comeremos, compraré, pasaré
any irregular verbs in the future tense	haremos	haremos
verbs referring to persons other than 'yo'	haremos, iremos, será	visitaremos, haremos, compraremos, comeremos
using the weather to talk about the future	si hace buen tiempo	si hace viento
si + present, + future	si hace buen tiempo, haremos una excursión al campo	si hace viento, practicaré el windsurf si tengo bastante dinero, compraré un helado

Page 39

Suggested answers

Una semana en mi ciudad

Mi ciudad está cerca del mar y es un puerto.

Hay muchas cosas para hacer, por ejemplo, se puede visitar el parque zoológico o ver la catedral.

Lo mejor de la ciudad es la comida. Hay restaurantes de todas partes del mundo. Lo malo es que hay mucho tráfico.

Durante la visita iremos a ver un partido de fútbol y, si hace buen tiempo, haremos una excursión en barco.

Mi área local

Mi pueblo está situado en las afueras de Londres, cerca del río.

En mi región el clima es variable. En invierno puede hacer bastante frío y en verano a veces llueve mucho.

El fin de semana pasado visité el museo de ciencias con mis padres. Vi cosas muy interesantes y aprendí mucho. Lo pasé muy bien.

El próximo fin de semana, si hace buen tiempo, podemos ir a un festival de música en el parque. Tocarán grupos durante toda la tarde. Podemos comer hamburguesas o pizza y por la noche habrá fuegos artificiales.

Page 40

Suggested answers

Los pros y contras de mi ciudad

En mi zona no hay mucho para los jóvenes. Solo hay un parque y un polideportivo, pero no hay piscina.

Lo mejor de mi ciudad es que hay un centro comercial con muchas tiendas y restaurantes. También hay una buena red de transporte para ir al centro.

Lo peor es que hay mucho tráfico y, por lo tanto, mucho ruido y contaminación. Es peligroso para la salud.

El fin de semana próximo, si llueve, tomaré el autobús para ir a cine con mis amigos. Si hace bueno, jugaré al fútbol en el parque.

¿Cómo es tu ciudad?

Mi zona es residencial, pero hay una calle principal con tiendas y cafeterías. También tiene un parque muy bonito donde paseo a mi perro.

En mi barrio se puede visitar el museo de la ciudad, que es muy interesante. También hay un mercado los sábados y se puede comprar comida y artículos de regalo.

El sábado pasado fui a la bolera con mis amigos. Jugamos un poco y luego comimos perritos calientes. Fue muy divertido y lo pasamos bien.

Durante el verano, si estoy en forma, participaré en una media maratón en mi zona. Será difícil pero gratificante.

Unit 6

Page 42

1

	fact(s)	example(s)	opinion(s)	reason(s)
• Año Nuevo	a party	–	likes it a lot	dances and sings
• días más importantes	Christmas Day New Year's Eve	–	special	presents prepared a celebration meal
• celebraciones durante el año	birthdays	birthdays	have a great time	invite whole family
• planes para ver fiestas	Feria de Abril in Sevilla next year	–	loves celebrations thinks it will be lovely	would like to see festivities in another country

2
- **a** porque
- **b** también
- **c** porque
- **d** pero
- **e** por ejemplo
- **f** además
- **g** creo que

Page 43

1
- **a** hace un mes (✗)
- **b** Semana Santa (✗)
- **c** ir al instituto (✗)
- **d** tomar el sol en la playa (✗)

2
- i present
- ii preterite
- iii present
- iv future

3 A f, B a, C b, D c, E d, F e

Page 44

1
- **a**
  - • ¿Qué hiciste para celebrar tu cumpleaños? 1, 3, 5, 8
  - • ¿Qué vas a hacer para celebrar tu próximo cumpleaños? 2, 4, 6, 7
- **b** 1, 3, 8, 5, 2, 4, 6, 7

2 ¿Cómo fue el festival de música?

bandas favoritas

entradas baratas

demasiado calor

acampar

¿Qué planes tienes para el verano que viene?

fiesta en España

desfiles bonitos

bailar en las calles

ropa típica

Page 45

1 A c, B d, C b, D a, E j, F g, G i, H f, I e, J h

2 Generalmente celebro mi cumpleaños con mi familia. Lo paso bien **porque** recibo regalos y tarjetas y **además** porque mi hermana me hace una tarta riquísima. **Sin embargo**, el año que viene quiero hacer algo diferente.

Mi cumpleaños es en verano; **por eso** voy a ir a un festival de música con mi mejor amiga. Lo pasaré bien **sobre todo** porque veré a mis grupos favoritos. Haremos camping y **por un lado** el ambiente será increíble, pero **por otro lado** no dormiré nada **ya que** el camping será muy ruidoso.

3
- **a** sin embargo
- **b** ya que
- **c** tampoco
- **d** sobre todo
- **e** por eso

Page 46

all points made are relevant to the bullets	• Año Nuevo	⊘ or examples from the text
		una fiesta comida toca una banda fuegos artificiales
	• días más importantes	Dia de Navidad – regalos, familia
	• celebraciones en familia	fiesta en casa barbacoa piscina
	• planes para ver fiestas	España ver fiestas en su pueblo hacer camping
use paragraphs		⊘
Keep all ideas addressing the same point together		⊘
Link ideas logically with connectives to…	add a fact	además, ya que
	give an alternative	–
	give an example	–
	create a contrast	sin embargo
	explain	porque, sobre todo
	add a consequence	por eso
	say 'if'	si es posible

Page 48

Suggested answer

Un festival de cine internacional

En las vacaciones del año pasado fui al festival de cine de Celalla. Se celebra en junio todos los años y las películas se ponen en varios lugares durante una semana.

Lo que más me gustó fue que todas las noches a las diez se ponía una película gratuita en la playa. ¡Fue guay!

Creo que los festivales son tan populares porque a la gente le gusta hacer actividades en grupo. Por ejemplo, mi hermano siempre va al festival de música en Reading, no solo porque le gusta la música, sino también porque le encanta divertirse con sus amigos.

En septiembre me gustaría asistir al festival de cine español en Londres porque me interesa aprender más sobre los directores españoles.

Unit 7

Page 50

① Amira works in a restaurant on Saturdays.

She's a waitress. She serves food and drinks to customers and sometimes helps in the kitchen.

Last Saturday she had to speak Spanish to two Argentinian customers.

She likes it because the customers are usually friendly. The negative aspect is that she doesn't have much free time.

Next year, she's going to do a course in tourism and she will do work experience in a hotel. In the future, she wants to be a flight attendant or a chef.

② a Trabajo los fines de semana
 b Me gusta el trabajo
 c tuve que hablar
 d comieron en el restaurante
 e voy a hacer un curso de turismo
 f haré prácticas

③ a camarera, azafata, cocinera
 b camarero, azafato, cocinero
 c They were women. The writer uses the word 'señoras' (not 'señores') and uses the feminine nationality adjective 'argentinas'.

Page 51

① A b
 B c
 C e
 D d
 E a

② a a B b D c C d A e E
 b a voy a trabajar b Estudiaré c Quiero ser/soy
  d pongo/quito/paso e Trabajé/Atendí
 c Suggested answers
  a 'Voy a trabajar…' answers question '¿Vas a trabajar…?' Uses near future tense
  b 'Estudiaré español…' answers question '¿Estudiarás idiomas el año que viene?' Uses future tense
  c 'Quiero ser ingeniero…' answers question '¿Qué trabajo quieres hacer?' Uses quiero + infinitive for talking about future plans

d 'Sí, pongo y quito la mesa...' answers question '¿Ayudas con las tareas en casa?' Uses present tense

e 'Trabajé en una agencia de viajes' answers question '¿Qué hiciste en tus prácticas laborales?' Uses preterite tense to talk about completed actions in the past

Page 52

(1) Correct verb forms in bold:

El verano pasado, **trabajé** en una granja de vacas. Mi amigo, Eduardo, también **trabajó** allí. Todos los días, **limpiamos** los establos. **Fue** un trabajo duro y sucio. Un día, las vacas **escaparon** pero el granjero **puso** un mensaje en WhatsApp y un vecino **contestó** en seguida. Eddie y yo **fuimos** a su granja y **encontramos** las vacas. ¡Menos mal!

(2) Correct possessive adjectives in bold:

Mi madre trabaja en una empresa pequeña. Le gusta porque **sus** compañeros son simpáticos y **su** jefe es agradable. **Mi** padre es profesor en una escuela primaria. Dice que **sus** alumnos son muy traviesos. Somos seis en casa porque tengo dos hermanos y **nuestra** abuela también vive con nosotros.

(3) (a) Me gusta trabajar en **el jardín porque** (b) me gusta estar **al aire libre.** (c) A mi padre **le gusta cocinar** (d) y a mi madre le **encanta limpiar.** (e) Pero no nos gusta **sacar la basura.**

Page 53

(1) **a** Spelling mistakes underlined:

Callum's text:

Trabajo en un garaje los <u>sabados</u> por la <u>manana</u>. Tengo que limpiar el suelo en el <u>taler</u> y lavar los coches. Soy bastante <u>practico</u> y me chiflan los coches. En el <u>future</u> quiero ser <u>mecanico</u> o ingeniero.

Bogdan's text:

El <u>ano</u> pasado, hice <u>practicas</u> laborales en una <u>officina</u>. Fue una experiencia <u>positive</u> y muy <u>util</u> porque aprendí a <u>attender</u> a los clientes.

b Corrections:

Callum's text: sábados, mañana, taller, práctico, futuro, mecánico

Bogdan's text: año, prácticas, oficina, positiva, útil, atender

(2) Corrected verbs with added accents in bold:

El mes pasado, hice mis prácticas laborales en un polideportivo. **Trabajé** en la recepción y en la oficina. Tuve que contestar el teléfono. También **mandé** correos electrónicos y **escribí** cartas. Fue una experiencia positiva y mi jefe en la oficina me **ayudó** mucho. El año que viene, **trabajaré** en un campamento de verano en España y al final, **hablaré** español bastante bien.

Page 54

(1) **a** trabajo, enseño, va, soy, es

b nadó, se quedó, hice, Saqué, archivé, no me gustó

c quiero ser

(2) activo, profesor

(3) una, contenta

(4) a / b

type of mistake	mistake	correction
incorrect use of capitals	Domingos	domingos
adjective doesn't agree with noun	pájaros pequeño	pájaros pequeños
possessive adjective doesn't agree with noun	su jardines	sus jardines
spelling mistake	sabados	sábados
wrong part of verb *gustar* used	me gusto la naturaleza	me gusta la naturaleza
wrong person of verb used	va a hacer	voy a hacer
wrong tense used	encuentro un nido	encontré un nido

Page 56

Suggested answer

Un campamento de verano

Estimado Señor:

Le escribo para solicitar un puesto de animador en el campamento de verano. Soy responsable, paciente y trabajador. Hablo inglés y estudio español y francés en el instituto. El mes pasado, hice un curso de primeros auxilios. Los fines de semana, hago de canguro y cuido a los niños de mis vecinos. Además, hice mis prácticas laborales en una escuela primaria donde ayudé en las clases de educación física y en las excursiones. En el futuro, me gustaría trabajar en el extranjero para conocer otros países y otras culturas.

Un cordial saludo:

Unit 8

Page 58

(1) Corrected words/phrases in bold:

a **La** contaminación del aire es un problema muy serio.

b **Hay** muchos sin hogar.

c Me **preocupa** el calentamiento global.

d No se debe tirar basura **al suelo.**

e El sábado pasado, **ayudé** a recoger botellas de plástico en el parque cerca **de** mi casa.

Page 59

(1) **a** / **b**

Mi hermano **[i] tiene** 24 años y trabaja de bombero. Explanation: Use *tener* with age, not *ser*.

Hoy hace sol y **[ii] hace** mucho calor. Explanation: Use *hacer* with weather, not *ser*.

Nuestro gato es muy delgado y siempre **[iii] tiene** hambre. Explanation: Use *tener* to express hunger.

José **[iv] toca** la guitarra bastante bien, pero juega muy mal al fútbol. Explanation: Use *tocar* to express 'to play' when referring to a musical instrument.

Sandra estudia inglés [v] **desde hace** cinco años. Explanation: Use *desde hace* + present tense to express how long you have been doing something.

② a de
  b de
  c En
  d por
  e a, en

Page 60

① a Los domingos, siempre **salgo** con mis amigos en bicicleta.

  b No tengo un trabajo, pero **cuido** al gato y al perro de nuestros vecinos cuando ellos se van de vacaciones.

  c Las tiendas de moda Zara y Mango **tienen** éxito en todo el mundo.

  d De lunes a viernes, **me levanto** a las siete menos cuarto.

  e Siempre **desayuno** un vaso de leche y pan tostado antes de ir al insti.

  f **Tienes** sueño porque te acostaste muy tarde anoche.

  g Mi amigo **tiene** suerte porque va de vacaciones a Cuba en enero.

  h Normalmente, en España **cenamos** entre las nueve y las diez.

  i Estoy contenta porque **saqué** buenas notas en idiomas y en matemáticas.

② a Tengo calor y tengo sed.
  b Tienen mucha suerte porque tienen un jardín grande.
  c Anoche, salí con mi familia.
  d Siempre desayunamos antes de ir al instituto.
  e Tim tiene que levantarse temprano porque es granjero.
  f Normalmente, saco buenas notas en inglés.

Page 61

① a un pueblo pequeño
  b muchos perros
  c demasiado pequeño
  d muchas plantas y flores
  e poco tráfico y muy poca contaminación
  f Nuestra casa
  g En nuestro jardín
  h Mis padres

② a No me gusta _ver_ basura en la calle.
  b Me gustaría _tomarme_ un año sabático.
  c Prefiero _trabajar_ en equipo.
  d El año que viene, vamos a _hacer_ un proyecto ecológico en el instituto.
  e En el futuro, quiero _estudiar_ geografía y estudios del medio ambiente.

A c
B a
C b
D e
E d

Page 62

① Corrections in bold:
  a Vivo en una **ciudad grande**.
  b Nos llevamos bien con **nuestros** vecinos.
  c Me gusta **vivir** en la ciudad porque mi casa está cerca **de** un parque.
  d El **mes pasado**, **reciclé** vidrio, papel y **muchas** botellas de plástico.
  e El año que viene, **mis** amigos y yo **vamos** a **organizar** un evento sobre la salud.

Page 63

① Suggested answers
  a Hace mucho calor en mi país.
  b Hay mucho tráfico.
  c Me preocupa la contaminación del aire.
  d El verano pasado, trabajé de voluntario y recogimos mucha basura.
  e En el futuro, quiero cuidar / proteger el medio ambiente.

Page 64

Suggested answers

Mi pueblo

a Vivo en un pueblo pequeño cerca de la playa.

b Hace mucho calor en julio y agosto.

c No hay mucho tráfico así que normalmente voy al instituto en bicicleta.

d La semana pasada, fuimos a Barcelona con nuestros profesores.

e El año que viene, vamos a organizar un torneo de fútbol para recaudar dinero.

La salud

a Creo que la salud es muy importante.

b Nunca fumo porque no es bueno para la salud.

c Llevamos una dieta sana en casa y practico / hago deporte todos los días.

d El fin de semana pasado participé en un evento deportivo solidario.

e El año que viene quiero participar en un medio maratón.

Unit 9

Page 66

① Ticked: **a, c, d, g**

  Corrected statements:
  b Teresa is also worried about rubbish.

(e) She thinks we can all play a part in protecting the environment.

(f) Teresa helped clean up her local park.

(h) She would like to volunteer in a tree-planting project because deforestation is a very serious problem.

②

Bullet points	Key points
los mayores problemas medioambientales en su barrio	la contaminación del aire, la basura
qué se debe hacer para resolver los problemas	reducir la contaminación, mejorar la red de transporte, ir en bici, no usar el coche, hacer campañas publicitarias, reciclar
lo que hizo para ser ecológico	participar en un proyecto, recogimos papeles y botellas
sus planes para ser solidario	estudiar ecología, trabajar como voluntario

Page 67

① Circled: medioambiental, la contaminación, la basura, los mares, los ríos, contaminar, cuidar, el medio ambiente, limpiar, ecología, destrucción

②
(a) la contaminación
(b) la basura
(c) contaminar
(d) hacer campañas publicitarias
(e) cuidar
(f) el medio ambiente
(g) participar
(h) el planeta
(i) la destrucción

③ **Af** – ahorrar agua

Be – separar la basura

Cc – comprar productos ecológicos

Dh – proteger el medio ambiente

Ea – reducir la contaminación

Fd – luchar contra el calentamiento global

Gg – apagar la luz

Hb – no usar bolsas de plástico

Page 69

① Suggested answers (others are possible)
(a) Para mí, lo más preocupante es el calentamiento global.
(b) Pienso que el problema más serio es la contaminación.
(c) Creo que se debería reducir la basura y reciclar más.
(d) En mi opinión, hay que hacer proyectos medioambientales.

②
(a) Creo que el problema más serio del planeta es la destrucción del medio ambiente. O En las

ciudades, hay contaminación del aire F+E y en los ríos y en el mar hay demasiada basura. F+E Además, hay miles de animales y plantas en peligro de extinción. F+E Pienso que todos tenemos que trabajar para proteger la naturaleza O porque si no lo hacemos ahora, no vamos a salvar el planeta. R Se debería hacer campañas publicitarias para animar a todos a ser más responsables O porque si todos lo hacemos, cambiaremos el mundo. R

(b) i creo que, pienso que

ii porque

iii además

Page 70

① (a) Circled: para mí, creo que, pienso que

(b) Highlighted: (i) trabajé como animador (en un curso de verano); hicimos actividades deportivas; (ii) había clases de cocina; (iii) vamos a participar (en un curso de música), terminará con (un concierto solidario)

② (a)/(b)

Problem (English)	Problem (Spanish)	Solution
unemployment	el desempleo / el paro	crear más oportunidades de trabajo
homeless people	la gente sin hogar	construir más pisos y casas de precio moderado
drug addiction and alcohol	la drogadicción y el alcohol	organizar campañas y proyectos para informar a la gente de los peligros de tomar drogas y beber alcohol

Page 72

Suggested answer

Un festival musical y medioambiental

Me gustaría trabajar como voluntario en el festival solidario porque que creo que la destrucción del medio ambiente es un problema muy serio. Lo que más me preocupa en mi ciudad es la contaminación del aire.

Me gustaría participar en el festival como voluntario porque creo que este evento puede recaudar dinero para proyectos medioambientales y que puede animar a la gente a actuar localmente. Tenemos que reducir el tráfico para mejorar la calidad del aire, y por eso, quiero contribuir a animar a la gente a ir más a pie, en bicicleta o en el transporte público.

Trabajo como voluntario en mi barrio. Soy miembro de un grupo ecologista que cuida las calles y las plazas. El año pasado, organizamos un medio maratón. Con el dinero que recaudamos, compramos árboles para el barrio.

En el futuro, vamos a organizar un mini-maratón para niños por zonas verdes, para promover el deporte, la salud y la protección del planeta.